Contents

How to use this book 2

Practice Papers: Set 1
- Paper 1 – Listening 5
- Paper 2 – Speaking 19
- Paper 3 – Reading 31
- Paper 4 – Writing 49

Practice Papers: Set 2
- Paper 1 – Listening 57
- Paper 2 – Speaking 71
- Paper 3 – Reading 83
- Paper 4 – Writing 99

Practice Papers: Set 3
- Paper 1 – Listening 107
- Paper 2 – Speaking 117
- Paper 3 – Reading 129
- Paper 4 – Writing 145

How to use this book

This book provides three sets of exam papers that mirror the AQA GCSE exam papers.

The audio, teacher-examiner parts (for Paper 2: Speaking), sample answers and mark schemes can be accessed using the QR codes throughout the book or by visiting http://www.oxfordsecondary.co.uk/aqagcse-german-pp.

The exam papers contain hints and tips. The first set of papers provides tips for all questions and all skills, in order to help you gain confidence in answering questions. In the second set of papers there are fewer tips for listening and reading. The third set of papers does not contain tips, so that you have an opportunity to practise answering questions independently in an exam situation.

AQA GCSE German Foundation

AQA GCSE German is made up of four exam papers, each with a weighting of 25% towards the final mark. The Foundation tier is for students targeting Grades 1-5. For more details about the specification and for the most up-to-date assessment information, please see the AQA website.

Paper 1: Listening

There are 35 minutes to complete the Foundation listening paper and 40 marks available. In Section A, the questions are in English and the answers required will either be non-verbal or in English. In Section B, the questions are in German and the answers required will either be non-verbal or in German.

The time includes 5 minutes at the start of the exam to read through the paper. Practise reading through the paper in this time. You may need to skim-read to get all the way through it, but try to use the time in a focused way. Identify the questions where you need to give several answers about the audio passage, or more than one piece of information, so that you're ready to listen out for the details you need. It's also good to read Section B carefully to make sure you understand the questions being asked.

The level of difficulty varies throughout the paper so don't lose heart if you encounter a hard question early on, as it doesn't mean you will find the questions that follow even harder. In AQA GCSE Paper 1, there are some questions that appear both on the Foundation and Higher tier papers.

Use the tips in the Set 1 and Set 2 listening papers in this book to build your confidence in exam technique and to help you listen out for the correct answers.

Paper 2: Speaking

There are 60 marks available for the speaking paper. For Foundation Tier, you will have supervised preparation time of 12 minutes followed by an exam of 7-9 minutes.

There are three parts to the exam:

- Role-play (15 marks) – this will last approximately 2 minutes for Foundation Tier
- Photo card (15 marks) – this will last approximately 2 minutes for Foundation Tier
- General Conversation (30 marks) – this will last between 3-5 minutes for Foundation Tier

The candidate chooses one theme for the general conversation and the other theme will be the one that hasn't been covered in the photo card. Here is a chart showing the possible test sequences based on the candidate's choice of theme:

Role-play	Candidate's chosen conversation theme	Photo card	Candidate's second conversation theme
1, 2 or 3	Theme 1: Identity and culture	B	Theme 3
		C	Theme 2
	Theme 2: Local, national, international and global areas of interest	A	Theme 3
		C	Theme 1
	Theme 3: Current and future study and employment	A	Theme 2
		B	Theme 1

Each paper in this book contains a role-play and a photo card from each theme. The teacher-examiner part and two marked sample responses for each can be found online. For general conversation, there are two marked sample responses included in the book for each paper, followed by tasks to complete, with the following combinations of themes:

- Set 1 covers Themes 1 and 2
- Set 2 covers Themes 2 and 3
- Set 3 covers Themes 3 and 1

Tips are provided for the role-plays and photo cards in the Set 1 and Set 2 speaking papers in this book. These will help you respond more fully to the questions asked and anticipate the unexpected questions.

Paper 3: Reading

There are 45 minutes to complete the Foundation reading paper, with 60 marks available. In Section A, the questions are in English and the answers required will either be non-verbal or in English. In Section B, the questions are in German and the answers required will either be non-verbal or in German. Different types of written texts are used in the reading paper, including literary extracts. In this book, example answers are given if further guidance is needed on how to answer a question, so watch out for these.

The level of difficulty varies throughout the paper so don't lose heart if you encounter a hard question early on, as it doesn't mean you will find the questions that follow even harder. In AQA GCSE Paper 3, there are some questions that appear both on the Foundation and Higher tier papers.

In Section C, there is a translation from German into English of a minimum of 35 words.

Use the tips in the Set 1 and Set 2 reading papers in this book to build your confidence in exam technique and to help you pick out the correct answers from the text.

Paper 4: Writing

There is 1 hour to complete the writing paper and 50 marks available. All answers should be written in German.

For Foundation Tier there are four questions:

- Question 1 (8 marks): this will require you to write four sentences about a photo.

- Question 2 (16 marks): 40 words are expected for this task, with a series of bullet points to cover in your response.

- Question 3 (10 marks): A translation from English into German of a minimum of 35 words.

- Question 4 (16 marks): One of a choice of two structured writing tasks of 90 words with a series of bullet points to cover in your response. In AQA GCSE Paper 4, this question is the same as question 1 on the Higher Tier paper.

Tips are provided in the Set 1 and Set 2 writing papers in this book, to help you respond to the questions and to give guidance on extending your answers. Two marked sample answers are included online for questions 2 and 4. Also included online is a mark scheme for question 3.

Practice Papers: Set 1

F

Foundation Tier Paper 1 Listening

Time allowed: 35 minutes
(including 5 minutes' reading time before the test)

You will need no other materials.
The pauses are pre-recorded for this test.

Information
- The marks for the questions are shown in brackets. The maximum mark for this paper is 40.
- You must **not** use a dictionary.

Advice
This is what you should do for each item.
- After the question number is announced, there will be a pause to allow you to read the instructions and questions.
- Listen carefully to the recording and read the questions again.
- Listen to the recording again, and then answer the questions.
- When the next question is about to start you will hear a bleep.
- You may write at any time during the test.
- In **Section A**, answer the questions in **English**. In **Section B**, answer the questions in **German**.
- You must answer all the questions in the spaces provided. Do not write on blank pages.
- Write neatly and put down all the information you are asked to give.
- **You must not ask questions or interrupt during the test.**
- You have five minutes to read through the question paper. You may make notes during this time. You may turn to the questions now.
- **The test starts now.**

Listen to the audio

Please note: The Practice Paper questions and answers have not been written or approved by AQA.

Practice Papers: Set 1

Section A Questions and answers in **English**

School subjects

Two Austrian teenagers are talking about school subjects. Write the correct letter in the box.

- Note down the German word for each subject pictured before you listen to the recording.
- Make sure you revise sets of words for common topics such as school subjects.

Which subject do they each like?

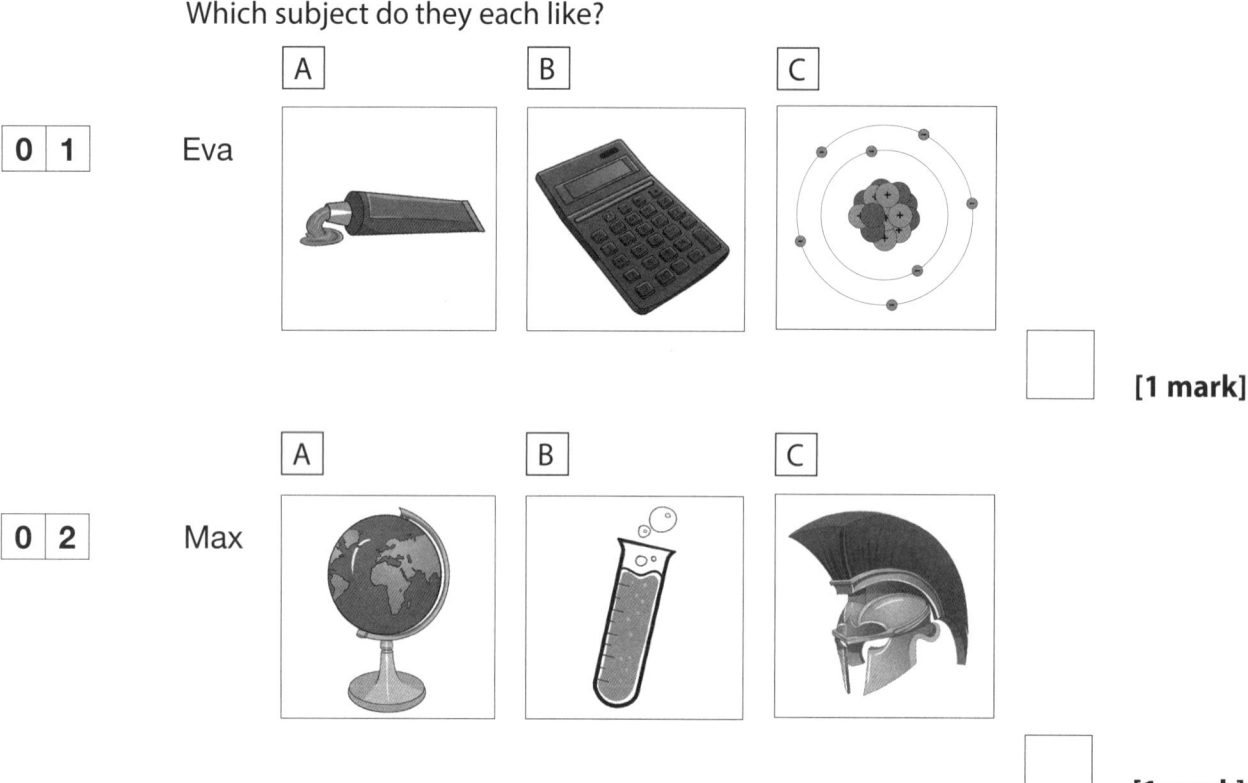

`0 1` Eva

[1 mark]

`0 2` Max

[1 mark]

Practice Papers: Set 1

Family members

Two people in a German café are talking about family members.

Answer both parts of the question in **English**.

> - Take care to distinguish between the German words for 'half brother' and 'brother'. You need to be very specific in your answers, otherwise you might not be awarded the mark.
> - Make use of the reading time at the start of the exam to identify tasks such as these, in which there are two questions based on one audio extract.

0 3 . 1 Who does the woman get on well with?

_____

[1 mark]

0 3 . 2 Why is the man worried about his sister?

_____

[1 mark]

Home town

Three Swiss teenagers are talking about where they live.

Which aspect of their town does each person like?

A	cafés
B	shopping centre
C	castle
D	noise
E	market
F	sports centre

> Listen out for the key noun in each statement. Don't get distracted by different ways of saying 'I like' or 'it's good'.

Write the correct letter in the box.

0 4 Sabine ☐ [1 mark]

0 5 Marko ☐ [1 mark]

0 6 Barbara ☐ [1 mark]

Festivals

Your German friend is telling you about Karneval.

0 7 Which **three** aspects of Karneval does she mention?

A	where Karneval takes place
B	how long Karneval lasts
C	the origins of Karneval
D	eating and drinking
E	dressing up
F	processions

> In this type of task, you will hear the options in the same order as the English list. Three of the options will not be mentioned.

Write the correct letters in the boxes.

☐ ☐ ☐ [3 marks]

Eating out

Christian and Anna are talking about eating out.

Write the correct letter in the box.

> In a multiple-choice task, all of the answers will be plausible, so keep an open mind until you have listened to the whole audio extract each time.

0 8 What was Christian's goulash like?

A	cold
B	delicious
C	good value

[1 mark]

0 9 Why does Anna rarely eat out?

A	She prefers cooking.
B	She is vegetarian.
C	She thinks it is too expensive.

[1 mark]

1 0 How often does Christian go to the restaurant he mentions?

A	once a week
B	once a fortnight
C	once a month

[1 mark]

Environmental problems

Three callers to a German phone-in programme are talking about environmental problems.

Answer the questions in **English**.

> - To avoid introducing errors when writing answers in English, don't give more information than is necessary.
> - Pay attention to singular and plural nouns: if you write and answer in the singular but the plural is required, you might not be awarded the mark.

1 1 Which problem does the first caller mention?

_____

[1 mark]

1 2 What does the second caller have to do every day?

_____

[1 mark]

1 3 What does the third caller complain about?

_____

[1 mark]

Careers

Your Swiss friend is talking about her plans for the future.

Answer **both** parts of the question.

Write the correct letter in the box.

> - Look for key words in the question that you might also hear in the recording. For example, in question 14.1, what is the German for 'younger'?
> - Think also about the tense you will need to listen out for. Question 14.1 is asking about which job Julia was interested in **in the past**.

14.1 When Julia was younger, which job interested her?

A	nurse
B	gardener
C	cook

[1 mark]

14.2 What does Julia say she must do?

A	go to university
B	do an apprenticeship
C	make lots of job applications

[1 mark]

Directions

A pedestrian asks for directions to the station.

Answer **both** parts of the question.

Write the correct letter in the box.

> - When a question includes numbers, you will not be required to make any calculations. The answer will always be stated in the audio.
> - Make sure you revise numbers. Making a mistake with large numbers is an easy way to lose marks.

15.1 Which way should she go first?

A (left arrow)   B (straight ahead)   C (right arrow)

[1 mark]

15.2 How far is it from here to the station?

A 200m   B 300m   C 500m

[1 mark]

Healthy living

A doctor is talking on Austrian radio about healthy living.

Answer all parts of the question in **English**.

> Listen out for negatives, which might include *nie* and *kein* as well as *nicht*.

16.1 What did the doctor do wrong in his younger days?

_____

[1 mark]

16.2 How often does he say people should play sport?

_____

[1 mark]

16.3 What does he say can happen if a person doesn't get enough sleep?

_____

[1 mark]

Holidays

Three German friends are talking about holidays.

Which aspect of a holiday does each person mention?

A	having an adventure
B	relaxing
C	seeing the sights
D	visiting friends
E	camping

Write the correct letter in the box.

> This task is not focusing on opinions, so ignore any opinions given and avoid letting them distract you from the key items of vocabulary you need to listen out for: the aspects of a holiday.

1 7 ☐ [1 mark]

1 8 ☐ [1 mark]

1 9 ☐ [1 mark]

Mobile phones

A German student is carrying out a survey about mobile phones.

Answer both parts of the question in **English**.

> Think of the different purposes people use their phones for, and make a note of these activities in German.

2 0 . 1 What does the first person use her mobile phone for?

_____

[1 mark]

2 0 . 2 What does the second person use his mobile phone for?

_____

[1 mark]

Marriage

Two Austrian students, Laura and Ben, are talking about marriage.

Fill in the blanks in the sentences below with a phrase in **English**.

> This item has a mixture of past, present and future tenses. Listen out for them carefully and make sure you answer in the correct tense in English – for example, the first question requires you to listen out for a past tense.

2 1 . 1 Two months ago, Laura's brother…

_____

[1 mark]

2 1 . 2 Ben's parents…

_____

[1 mark]

2 1 . 3 Laura's grandparents…

_____

[1 mark]

2 1 . 4 Ben thinks that it's important to…

_____

[1 mark]

Practice Papers: Set 1

Section B Questions and answers in **German**

Freunde

Erika spricht über ihre Freunde.

> Look first at the differences between the pictures and think carefully about the adjectives you are likely to hear.

2 2 Wie ist Erikas beste Freundin?

Schreib den richtigen Buchstaben in das Kästchen. ☐ **[1 mark]**

Das Wetter

Du hörst einen Wetterbericht.

> Listen out specifically for *im Süden* in the recording and don't be distracted by irrelevant information.

2 3 Wie wird das Wetter im Süden sein?

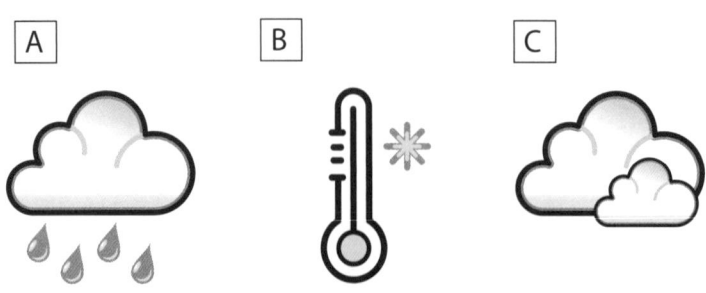

Schreib den richtigen Buchstaben in das Kästchen. ☐ **[1 mark]**

Nach der Schulzeit

Matthias spricht über seine Pläne.

> - You will hear all four answer options mentioned but listen carefully to identify which activities Matthias says he intends to do.
> - Not everything you hear will relate to Matthias and remember too that negatives change the meaning of a sentence.

2 4 Was wird Matthias nach der Schulzeit machen?

A	auf die Uni gehen
B	reisen
C	eine Ausbildung machen
D	in Hamburg arbeiten

Schreib die richtigen Buchstaben in die Kästchen.

☐ ☐

[2 marks]

Probleme in der Familie

Lina spricht über zwei Familienmitglieder, die Probleme haben.

Welche Probleme haben sie? Was sind die Konsequenzen?

Füll die Tabelle auf **Deutsch** aus.

> Each statement includes a time phrase, but you don't have to include these in your answer. Use single words or short phrases to convey the key points and avoid giving irrelevant details.

2 5 der Onkel

Problem	Konsequenz

[2 marks]

2 6 die Kusine

Problem	Konsequenz

[2 marks]

END OF QUESTIONS

Answers and mark schemes

Practice Papers: Set 1

AQA GCSE German (9-1)

PRACTICE PAPER F

Foundation Tier Paper 2 Speaking

Time allowed: 7–9 minutes
(+12 minutes' supervised preparation time)

Candidate's material – Role-play and Photo card

Instructions
- During the preparation time you must prepare the Role-play card and Photo card stimulus cards given to you.
- You may make notes during the preparation time on the paper provided by your teacher-examiner. Do not write on the stimulus cards.
- Hand your notes and both stimulus cards to the teacher-examiner before the General Conversation.
- You must ask the teacher-examiner at least one question in the General Conversation.

Information
- The test will last a maximum of 9 minutes and will consist of a Role-play (approximately 2 minutes) and a Photo card (approximately 2 minutes), followed by a General Conversation (3–5 minutes) based on your nominated Theme and the remaining Theme which has not been covered in the Photo card.
- You must **not** use a dictionary at any time during the test. This includes the preparation time.

Teacher's scripts

Please note: The Practice Paper questions and answers have not been written or approved by AQA.

AQA GCSE German Foundation Practice Papers © Oxford University Press 2020. Photocopying prohibited.

Practice Papers: Set 1

ROLE-PLAY 1

CANDIDATE'S ROLE

Part 1

Instructions to candidates

Your teacher will play the part of your Swiss friend and will speak first.

You should address your friend as *du*.

When you see this – **!** – you will have to respond to something you have not prepared.

When you see this – **?** – you will have to ask a question.

Du sprichst mit deinem Freund / deiner Freundin aus der Schweiz über deine Stadt.

- Deine Stadt (**zwei** Details).
- **!**
- Stadtmitte – wie oft.
- Die öffentlichen Verkehrsmittel – Meinung.
- **?** Geschäfte.

- If the task specifies **zwei** *Details*, make sure that you include two appropriate details. Don't try to give more than two, to avoid introducing incorrect language.
- You have just made a brief comment on your town. Think about which follow-up questions the teacher-examiner might ask, requiring an answer that is more than just *ja* or *nein*.
- You could use the word for 'every' to address the third bullet, or you could specify a day of the week with *am*.
- In the GCSE exam it is important to express opinions clearly. Don't be too ambitious but stick to an opinion that you know how to say in German.
- No question word is specified for the last bullet, so you can ask any question that refers to shops or shopping. Remember that you are addressing your friend, so you must use the *du* form.

ROLE-PLAY 2

CANDIDATE'S ROLE

Part 1

Instructions to candidates

Your teacher will play the part of the receptionist and will speak first.

You should address the receptionist as *Sie*.

When you see this – **!** – you will have to respond to something you have not prepared.

When you see this – **?** – you will have to ask a question.

Sie sprechen mit dem Rezeptionisten / der Rezeptionistin in einem Sportzentrum in Deutschland.

- Reservierung – Name und Sport.
- Zum Sportzentrum kommen – wie oft.
- Sportzentrum – Meinung.
- **?** Preis.
- **!**

- Read the role-play scenario carefully at the start of the preparation time so you are clear where the role-play takes place.
- Give your name – there is no need to spell it out – and then choose an appropriate sport that you know how to say in German.
- Revise question words and make sure you know when they are used. Choose an appropriate time phrase for the second bullet point, perhaps beginning with the German for 'every'.
- Think of a straightforward opinion for the third question, perhaps that you find the sports centre modern or clean.
- How do we say 'What does it cost?' Make sure you know how to form questions as you will need to ask one.
- A general question about sport or the sports centre is likely for the unexpected question.

ROLE-PLAY 3

CANDIDATE'S ROLE

Part 1

Instructions to candidates

Your teacher will play the part of your Austrian friend and will speak first.

You should address your friend as *du*.

When you see this – **!** – you will have to respond to something you have not prepared.

When you see this – **?** – you will have to ask a question.

> Du sprichst mit deinem Freund / deiner Freundin aus Österreich über deine Schule.
>
> - Dein Schultag (**zwei** Details).
> - **!**
> - AGs an deiner Schule (**zwei** Details).
> - Mittagspause (**eine** Aktivität).
> - **?** Hausaufgaben

- Keep the first answer as simple as possible, especially because you are required to say two things. Number and length of lessons would be appropriate, as would the starting and finishing times of the school day.
- Think what else might be asked about school for the unexpected question. A question on school subjects is likely.
- Don't try to translate the name of a school club into German for the third question. It is probably easier to say which activities you can do, e.g. *Man kann…*
- Pay attention to singular and plural nouns: you are asked about *AGs* in the third question and you need to give two details.
- Use a verb that you are familiar with for the fourth question but avoid repeating the answer you gave for the previous prompt. In this role-play you asked for a number of different details. Use your preparation time to write down exactly what you are going to say.
- Make sure to use a verb when asking the question, to ensure it is fully communicated.

Card A	**Candidate's Photo card**
Part 2	

- Look at the photo during the preparation period.
- Make any notes you wish to on an additional piece of paper.
- Your teacher will then ask you questions about the photo and about topics related to **me, my family and friends.**

Your teacher will ask you the following three questions and then **two more questions** which you have not prepared.

- Was gibt es auf dem Foto?
- Beschreib deinen idealen Partner / deine ideale Partnerin.
- Möchtest du in Zukunft heiraten? … Warum (nicht)?

> - Think of some phrases that could be applied to any photo such as *Im Hintergrund sieht man…* and *Im Vordergrund gibt es…*
> - The second question gives you the chance to use appropriate adjectives to describe personality.
> - Even if marriage is something you have never thought about, it is best to go for a definite 'yes' or 'no', followed by a suitable reason. Giving a reason will lead to higher marks.
> - Since the topic is given as 'me, my family and friends', the two unseen questions are likely to go beyond marriage and deal with other aspects of family and friends. Prepare some notes on your family and friends, writing down key words that you have learnt during the course.

Practice Papers: Set 1

Card B   **Candidate's Photo card**

Part 2

- Look at the photo during the preparation period.
- Make any notes you wish to on an additional piece of paper.
- Your teacher will then ask you questions about the photo and about topics related to **social issues**.

Your teacher will ask you the following three questions and then **two more questions** which you have not prepared.

- Was gibt es auf dem Foto?
- Wie findest du gesundes Essen?
- Was wirst du in Zukunft machen, um fit zu sein?

> - Try to prepare answers of at least three sentences, using a verb in each one.
> - You could say who you think the two people are in the photo. You could also say what they are doing and which room they are in.
> - Try to give a specific answer for the second question rather than just *gut*. You could, for example, use the verb *schmecken* and perhaps the adjective *billig* or its opposite, *teuer*.
> - Rather than saying more about your diet for the third question, you could comment on what sport and exercise you might undertake in the future, as well as talking about sleep and the avoidance of stress.
> - The topic is given as 'social issues', which is very broad. However, the two unseen questions might still refer to other aspects of health, such as the avoidance of smoking, drugs and alcohol.

Card C   **Candidate's Photo card**

Part 2

- Look at the photo during the preparation period.
- Make any notes you wish to on an additional piece of paper.
- Your teacher will then ask you questions about the photo and about topics related to **my studies**.

Your teacher will ask you the following three questions and then **two more questions** which you have not prepared.

- Was gibt es auf dem Foto?
- Wie findest du Mathe? … Warum?
- Was hast du letzte Woche im Unterricht gemacht?

> - Most photos in the exam will include people. In this one, you could say who the people are, where they are, and what subject is being taught.
> - In answer to *warum* in the second question, you could use a clause beginning with *weil*, remembering to send the verb to the end of the sentence.
> - Pay attention to the tense of the question that you are being asked so you give a response in the appropriate tense. In response to the third question, you need to use at least one verb in the perfect tense. Don't try to give too much detail; just keep to familiar ideas and language.
> - The two unseen questions could relate to other aspects of school life such as homework, clubs and activities. If you gave fully-developed answers to the first three questions, you can afford to be briefer here.
> - Remember to focus carefully on good pronunciation when giving your answers.

GENERAL CONVERSATION

Part 3

The Photo card is followed by a General Conversation. The first part of the conversation will be on a theme nominated by the candidate and the second part on the other theme not covered by the Photo card. The total time for the General Conversation will be between **three and five minutes** and a similar amount of time should be spent on each theme. Here is a reminder of the three themes:

- Identity and culture
- Local, national, international and global areas of interest
- Current and future study and employment

The following pages show two examples of the general conversation with accompanying commentary on how these conversations would be marked, followed by tasks.

Conversation 1: Themes 1 and 2

Jetzt die Konversation. Zuerst Thema 1. Wie alt bist du?
Fünfzehn.

Wann hast du Geburtstag?
Im Oktober.

Was für eine Person bist du?
Ich bin freundlich.

Verstehst du dich gut mit deiner Familie?
Ja. Meine Mutter hat immer Zeit für mich, und meine Schwester ist freundlich.

Hast du Tanten und Onkel?
Ja. Ich habe einen Onkel und eine Tante.

Ist Heiraten wichtig für dich?
Ja.

Wie ist deine ideale Partnerin oder dein idealer Partner?
Mein idealer Partner ist freundlich.

Hörst du gern Musik?
Ja. Ich höre jeden Tag Musik.

Was siehst du gern im Fernsehen?
Musiksendungen.

Hast du eine Frage für mich?
Ja. Haben Sie Geschwister?

Ja, ich habe eine Schwester. Und jetzt machen wir Thema 2. Wo wohnst du?
Ich wohne in einem Haus am Stadtrand.

Magst du dein Haus?
Ja, ich finde mein Haus schön. Ich habe mein eigenes Zimmer.

Was hast du in deinem Zimmer?
Einen Schreibtisch und einen Kleiderschrank.

Wie ist dein ideales Haus?
Mein ideales Haus ist groß und hat ein Schwimmbad.

Wie findest du deine Stadt?
Meine Stadt ist interessant.

Wie ist das Wetter in deiner Gegend?
Es regnet oft.

Wie gesund lebst du?
Ich esse viel Obst und Gemüse.

Treibst du auch Sport?
Ja. Ich treibe viel Sport.

Was hast du letzte Woche gemacht, um fit zu bleiben?
Ich spiele Federball und Hockey.

Marks and commentary

	Communication	Range and accuracy of language	Pronunciation and intonation	Spontaneity and fluency	Total
Marks	5/10	6/10	3/5	3/5	**17/30**

The conversation has been awarded 5 marks for Communication, as only short responses are given, some of which do not include a verb. An opinion is successfully conveyed in response to the question *Magst du dein Haus?* and an appropriate question is asked of the teacher-examiner, but only when prompted.

A mark of 6 has been awarded for Range and accuracy of language because basic language is used, with only simple structures such as present tense verbs. There are no successful references to past or future time frames: although the teacher-examiner asks one question about the past, referring to keeping fit last week, the response is in the present tense. For this reason, a higher mark cannot be given.

It is assumed that the pronunciation is largely intelligible but with little attempt at intonation. There may be difficulties with umlauts and the vowels *ei* and *ie*.

It is assumed that there are frequent hesitations and that delivery is generally slow. A few responses may be more fluent but the lack of intonation suggests that they have been pre-learnt. This results in a mark of 3 for Spontaneity and fluency.

> 1. **Try to give more detail by inserting an appropriate adjective into each of the following phrases. Use a different adjective each time and pay attention to the endings:**
>
>   a) *Ich wohne in einem … Haus.*
>   b) *(Ich habe) einen … Schreibtisch.*
>   c) *Mein ideales Haus hat ein … Schwimmbad.*
>
> 2. **How could you develop the short responses in the first nine questions? For example, in the first answer, you could give a full sentence** *(Ich bin fünfzehn Jahre alt)* **and then you could volunteer your birthday** *(Ich habe im Oktober Geburtstag)*, **in which case, the teacher-examiner would not need to ask the next question.**

Conversation 2: Themes 1 and 2

Jetzt die Konversation. Zuerst Thema 1. Wie alt bist du?
Ich bin fünfzehn Jahre alt. Ich habe im August Geburtstag.

Was für eine Person bist du?
Ich bin immer freundlich, aber manchmal faul. Ich habe viele Freunde.

Verstehst du dich gut mit deiner Familie?
Ja. Meine Mutter hat immer Zeit für mich, und meine Schwester hat dieselben Interessen wie ich.

Hast du Tanten und Onkel?
Ja. Mein Onkel wohnt in dieser Stadt, und wir treffen uns oft. Letztes Wochenende sind wir zusammen ins Kino gegangen. Ich habe auch eine Tante, aber sie wohnt in Südamerika, und ich sehe sie selten.

Ist Heiraten wichtig für dich?
Ja. Ich möchte heiraten, wenn ich älter bin.

Wie ist deine ideale Partnerin oder dein idealer Partner?
Mein idealer Partner ist aktiv und humorvoll.

Hörst du gern Musik?
Ja. Ich höre jeden Tag Musik. Ich spiele auch Gitarre mit meinen Freunden. Das macht Spaß.

Was siehst du gern im Fernsehen?
Ich sehe manchmal Musiksendungen. Ich mag auch die Sportschau. Gestern Abend habe ich ein wichtiges Fußballspiel gesehen. Sehen Sie gern Sport im Fernsehen?

Ja, sehr gern. Und jetzt machen wir Thema 2. Wo wohnst du?
Ich wohne in einem kleinen Haus am Stadtrand.

Magst du dein Haus?
Ja, ich finde mein Haus schön. Ich habe mein eigenes Zimmer. An der Wand habe ich viele Poster von meiner Lieblingssängerin.

Wie ist dein ideales Haus?
Mein ideales Haus ist groß und hat ein Schwimmbad. Ich gehe sehr gern schwimmen.

Wie findest du deine Stadt?
Meine Stadt ist interessant. Wir haben einen guten Markt und ein altes Schloss. Es gibt auch ein neues Einkaufszentrum in der Stadtmitte.

Wie ist das Wetter in deiner Gegend?
Es regnet oft. Gestern hat es den ganzen Tag geregnet. Aber im Sommer ist es ziemlich warm. Man kann dann im Garten sitzen.

Wie gesund lebst du?
Meine Gesundheit ist sehr wichtig. Ich esse viel Obst und Gemüse. Ich treibe viel Sport. Und natürlich trinke ich keinen Alkohol.

Was hast du letzte Woche gemacht, um fit zu bleiben?
Ich habe Federball gespielt, und ich bin auch Radgefahren. Ich habe gar nicht am Computer gespielt.

Marks and commentary

	Communication	Range and accuracy of language	Pronunciation and intonation	Spontaneity and fluency	Total
Marks	10/10	10/10	5/5	5/5	**30/30**

The conversation scores full marks for Communication: some extended responses are given where appropriate, for example, when talking about the weather, an additional comment is made about both the rain and the temperature. Information and opinions are conveyed clearly and opinions are explained. For example, in response to the question about their home town, an explanation is given as to why it is an interesting place. An appropriate question of the teacher-examiner is asked spontaneously, without needing to be prompted.

The full 10 marks have been awarded for Range and accuracy of language because a good variety of linguistic structures is used, with no unnecessary repetition. There are some examples of complex language, such as the phrase *dieselben Interessen wie ich* and the *wenn*-clause in the response about marriage. The future is referred to successfully when talking about marriage, as is the past when talking about last night's football match, yesterday's weather and what they did last week to keep fit.

It is assumed that the pronunciation and intonation are generally good but with some inconsistency at times. Minor errors might include the vowels in *ideales* and the *z* in *ziemlich*.

It is assumed that a suitable pace is maintained, but with some hesitations, especially in longer responses. Despite the hesitations, the conversation would still gain 5 marks for Spontaneity and fluency.

> 1. Make a list of the adjectives that have been used. Then try substituting other adjectives that you know. For example, instead of saying *Meine Stadt ist interessant*, you could say *Meine Stadt ist faszinierend*.
>
> 2. Look back at the responses that are made up of two or more sentences. Then think of other ways in which these responses could be developed with more complex language structures. For example, following the answer *Es gibt auch ein neues Einkaufszentrum in der Stadtmitte*, you could say something like *wo ich am Wochenende Kleider kaufe*.

Model answers and mark schemes

Practice Papers: Set 1

AQA GCSE German (9-1)

Foundation Tier Paper 3 Reading

Time allowed: 45 minutes

Instructions
- Answer **all** questions.
- Answer the questions in the spaces provided.
- In **Section A**, answer the questions in **English**. In **Section B**, answer the questions in **German**. In **Section C**, translate the passage into **English**.
- Cross through any work you do not want to be marked.

Information
- The marks for the questions are shown in brackets.
- The maximum mark for this paper is 60.
- You must **not** use a dictionary.

Please note: The Practice Paper questions and answers have not been written or approved by AQA.

Practice Papers: Set 1

Section A Questions and answers in **English**

| 0 | 1 | **Family**

Paul's mother has messaged him to say that she is not at home.

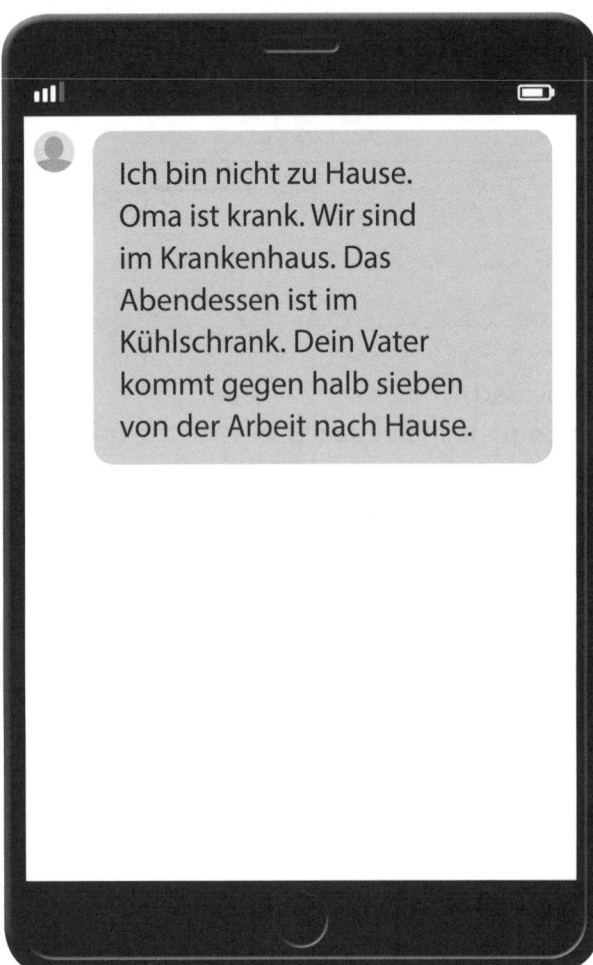

Ich bin nicht zu Hause. Oma ist krank. Wir sind im Krankenhaus. Das Abendessen ist im Kühlschrank. Dein Vater kommt gegen halb sieben von der Arbeit nach Hause.

- Be careful with times of the day. The 24-hour clock is used in the answers but not in the original text.
- Think carefully about the German way of talking about the time: half **past** the hour in English is seen as halfway **towards** the next hour in German.

Write the correct letter in the box.

| 0 | 1 | . | 1 | Where is Paul's mother?

A	at Grandma's house
B	at work
C	at the hospital

[1 mark]

▶ Continued

0 1 . 2 Where will Paul find the evening meal?

A	in the fridge
B	in the oven
C	in the kitchen cupboard

[1 mark]

0 1 . 3 When will Paul's father be home?

A	17:30
B	18:30
C	19:30

[1 mark]

0 2   **Part-time work**

You read this job advert.

Answer the questions in **English**.

> **Tierheim**
> Hast du sonntagnachmittags Zeit? Liebst du Hunde? Wir suchen Tierfans, die mit unseren Hunden spielen. Die Arbeit ist freiwillig, aber die Helfer bekommen immer Kuchen.

> Your answers can be short, but must each include **two** details. You must have **at least** two words for each answer. However, the answer to question 2.1 can be found in just one German word (*sonntagnachmittags*) because of the way German combines words.

0 2 . 1   When do you need to be available to work? Give **two** details.

_____

[2 marks]

0 2 . 2   What does the work involve? Give **two** details.

_____

[2 marks]

0 2 . 3   What does the advert say about pay? Give **two** details.

_____

_____

[2 marks]

0 3 **Free-time activity**

You read this poster on a notice board.

Answer the questions in **English**.

> **Freizeitklub**
> Unser Klub ist für Rentner, die allein leben und Kontakt suchen. Wir treffen uns zweimal im Monat, um Federball zu spielen. Sind Sie nicht sehr aktiv? Für Sie gibt es auch Schach.

Never leave an answer blank. If you don't know what an item of vocabulary means, guess from the context. It might just be correct!

0 3 . 1 The club is aimed at people who live alone and want to meet others. What else do we know about these people?

_____

[1 mark]

0 3 . 2 How often do they meet?

_____

[1 mark]

0 3 . 3 Which **two** activities are offered?

_____

_____

[2 marks]

04 School

Read Mia's blog about school.

Answer the questions in **English**.

> Viele Schüler in meiner Klasse sind faul. In der Pause gehen sie in soziale Medien und kommen spät in den Unterricht. Meiner Meinung nach ist das doof.
>
> Ich bin fleißiger, weil ich gute Noten bekommen will. Ich will Ärztin werden.

- You don't need to answer in full sentences.
- You will find the answers in order as you read through the text.
- Remember to answer in the correct language. Question 4.1 asks which adjective Mia uses, but you need to give the English translation.

04.1 Which adjective does Mia use to describe the other students in her class?

_____

[1 mark]

04.2 What do the students during break?

_____

[1 mark]

04.3 What is Mia's opinion of her classmates' behaviour?

_____

[1 mark]

04.4 Why does Mia try to get good marks?

_____

[1 mark]

0 5 A celebration

Read Nicole's post.

> Am Donnerstag den 22. Oktober habe ich meinen sechzehnten Geburtstag gefeiert. Meine Party hat viel Spaß gemacht. Ein großes Dankeschön an euch alle für die tollen Geschenke. Ich habe Glück, dass ich so viele lustige Freunde habe. Seht euch die Fotos an!

Look carefully at the tense used in each sentence. This will help you work out the correct answers for questions 5.2 and 5.3.

Write the correct letter in the box.

0 5 . 1 The 22nd October is a…

A	Tuesday.
B	Wednesday.
C	Thursday.

[1 mark]

0 5 . 2 The celebration…

A	will take place soon.
B	has already taken place.
C	is taking place today.

[1 mark]

0 5 . 3 Nicole is posting to…

A	invite her friends to a party.
B	say thank you for coming to her party.
C	say thank you for her presents.

[1 mark]

0 5 . 4 Nicole describes her friends as…

A	funny.
B	lucky.
C	happy.

[1 mark]

0 6 Environment

Read the responses of five teenagers to an online post about what their families do for the environment.

Write the first letter of the correct name in the box.

Write **S** for Salma.

Write **K** for Klara.

Write **T** for Thomas.

Write **A** for Annelie.

Write **P** for Peter.

> In this question there are five people, but only four questions. The text which is not used for an answer will contain elements which are similar to words you are looking for. For example, there are references to cars in both Klara's and Peter's comments, so look carefully at the details to work out the correct answer to question 6.3.

Salma
Meine Eltern wollen Solarzellen auf dem Dach haben. Sie meinen, wir benutzen zu viel Energie, denn jeder in unserer Familie hat einen Laptop, ein Handy und einen Fernseher.

Klara
Viele Menschen fahren zu schnell auf der Autobahn. Das ist umweltfeindlich. Sie sollten lieber mit dem Bus oder mit der Bahn fahren.

Thomas
Zu Hause trennen wir den Müll. Das ist gut, aber meine Schwester isst sehr viel Fastfood. Deshalb bringt sie immer zu viel Plastik und Verpackung ins Haus.

Annelie
Wir kaufen nur die Lebensmittel, die wir wirklich brauchen. Wir wollen kein Essen wegwerfen. An zwei Tagen der Woche essen wir jetzt kein Fleisch mehr.

Peter
Benzin ist teuer und Abgase sind schädlich. Also hat meine Mutter ein Elektroauto gekauft. Meiner Meinung nach ist es zu klein und zu langsam.

▶ Continued

| 0 6 . 1 | Who separates his/her rubbish? | | **[1 mark]** |

| 0 6 . 2 | Who has changed his/her diet? | | **[1 mark]** |

| 0 6 . 3 | Who would prefer a faster car? | | **[1 mark]** |

| 0 6 . 4 | Whose parents are concerned about electricity usage? | | **[1 mark]** |

07 **Healthy lifestyles**

Read the comments by three teenagers on social media about their lifestyles.

Write the **four** correct details in the grid.

> Take care to spot which tenses are being used. Don't assume that the texts will use tenses in the same order as in the grid.

Julia
Heute esse ich keinen Zucker. Als Kleinkind habe ich ziemlich ungesund gelebt. Meine Oma hat mir zu viele Süßigkeiten gegeben. Wenn ich Kinder habe, werde ich gesundes Essen für sie kochen.

Max
In Zukunft werde ich mehr Sport treiben. Mein Lebensstil ist nicht so gesund, weil ich so wenig Zeit habe. Früher bin ich viel öfter Rad gefahren.

Anton
Das Wichtigste ist, dass man viel Wasser trinkt. Letztes Jahr habe ich nur Cola getrunken. Jetzt trinke ich zwei Liter Wasser pro Tag. Meine älteren Freunde trinken Alkohol, aber das werde ich nie tun.

	Past	Present	Future
Julia	lived quite unhealthily		cook healthy food
Max		doesn't have much time	do more sport
Anton		drinks two litres of water a day	

[4 marks]

0 8 Festivals

Read this extract about festivals from Michael's diary.

> Weihnachten ist ein wichtiges Fest bei mir zu Hause. Meine Familie liebt die Traditionen, und wir haben immer einen Adventskranz im Esszimmer. Da meine Eltern meine Großeltern einladen, muss ich ein Zimmer mit meinem jüngeren Bruder teilen. Das hasse ich.
>
> Viele Familien schmücken den Weihnachtsbaum am Heiligen Abend. Wir schmücken ihn aber schon eine Woche früher, weil meine Schwester so ungeduldig ist. Ich finde meine Schwester verrückt.
>
> Obwohl meine Eltern und Geschwister Weihnachten genießen, dauert das Fest einfach viel zu lange für mich. Deshalb ist mein Lieblingsfest Silvester. Dann ist Weihnachten endlich vorbei und das normale Leben kann wieder anfangen.

Which **four** statements are true?

> The statements may not be exact translations of sentences in the text and you might have to infer information. For example, think about another English way of saying 'means a lot' in statement A, then see if you can find this at the start of the text.

A	Christmas means a lot to Michael's family.
B	Michael's family have an advent wreath in the living room.
C	He usually goes to his grandparents' house for Christmas.
D	Michael doesn't enjoy sharing a room with his brother.
E	His family always decorates the Christmas tree on Christmas Eve.
F	He thinks his sister is crazy.
G	Michael enjoys Christmas less than his family.
H	He always goes to a New Year's Eve party.

Write the correct letters in the boxes.

[4 marks]

Section B Questions and answers in **German**

0 9 **Skifahren**

Lies die E-Mail.

Beantworte die Fragen auf **Deutsch**.

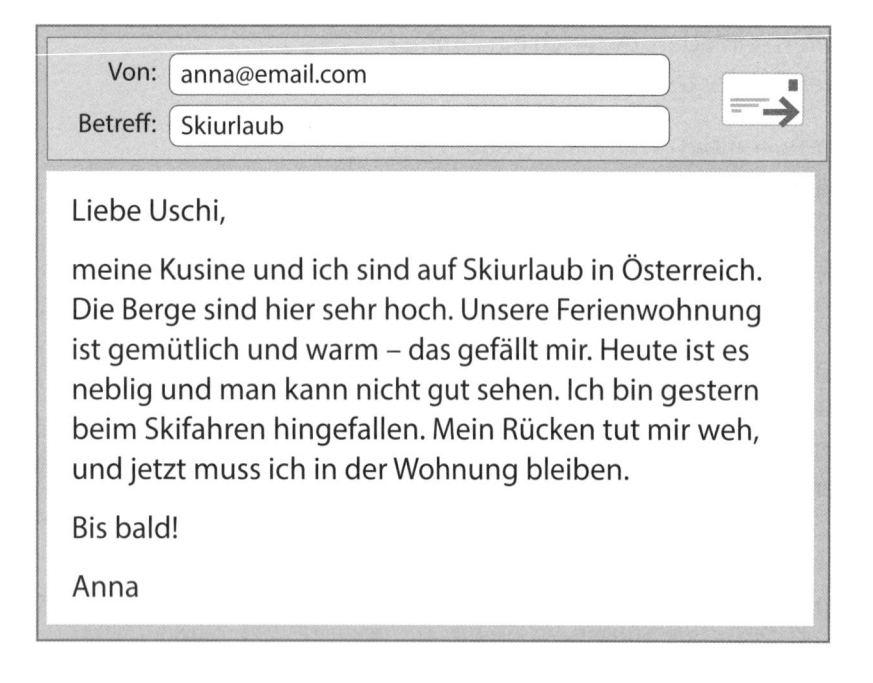

Von: anna@email.com
Betreff: Skiurlaub

Liebe Uschi,

meine Kusine und ich sind auf Skiurlaub in Österreich. Die Berge sind hier sehr hoch. Unsere Ferienwohnung ist gemütlich und warm – das gefällt mir. Heute ist es neblig und man kann nicht gut sehen. Ich bin gestern beim Skifahren hingefallen. Mein Rücken tut mir weh, und jetzt muss ich in der Wohnung bleiben.

Bis bald!

Anna

> Question 9.1 asks you about the weather. You can see the word *warm* in the text, but check what else is in the sentence to see if it is the weather which is mentioned here. Look at the next sentence to find another adjective which can only describe weather.

0 9 . 1 Wie ist das Wetter?

_____

[1 mark]

0 9 . 2 Wo hat Anna sich verletzt?

_____

[1 mark]

1 0 **Im Restaurant**

Lies die Online-Diskussion über ein Restaurant.

Schreib die richtigen Buchstaben in die Kästchen.

Schreib **C** für Carla.

Schreib **N** für Noah.

Schreib **F** für Felix.

Schreib **G** für Gabi.

Schreib **L** für Leon.

> None of the nouns in the questions appear in the text. Instead, you will find German examples of those things: for example, in question 10.1 you need to look for the name of a meat dish.

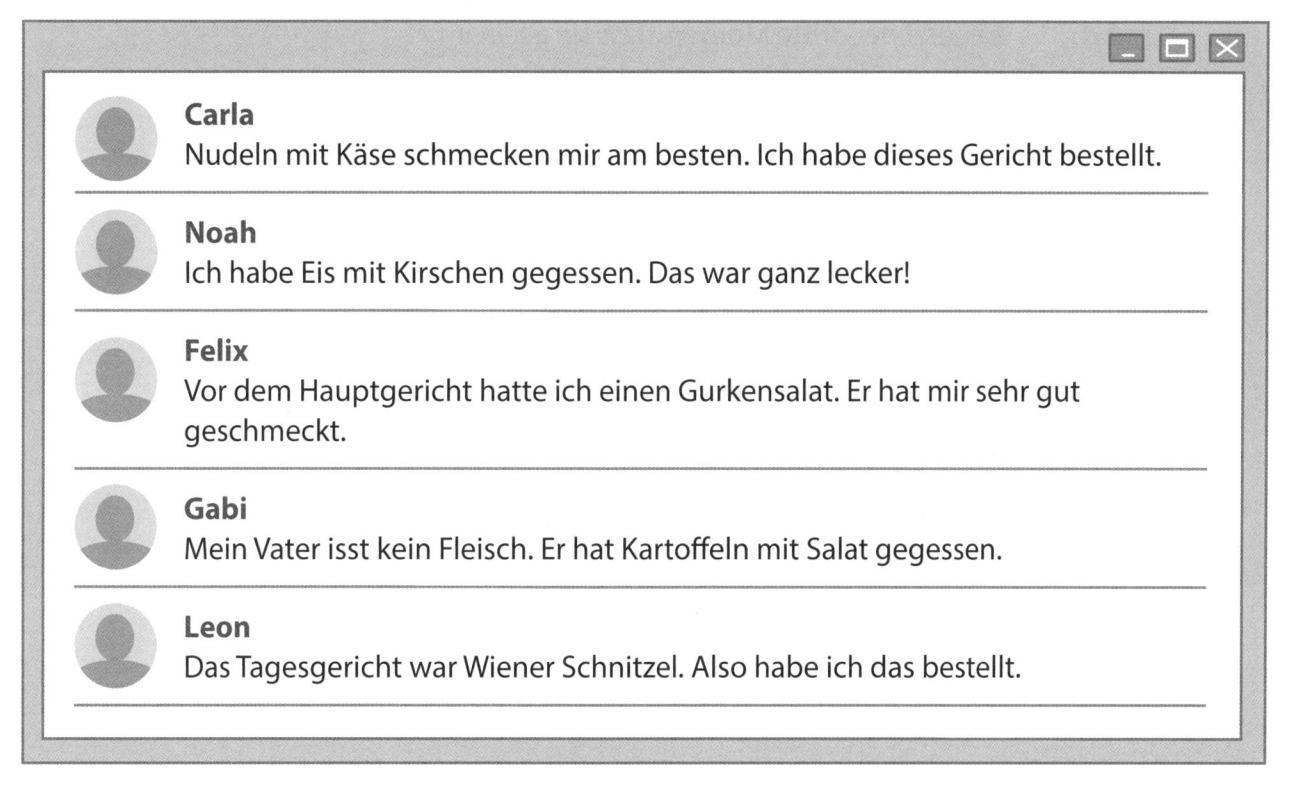

Carla
Nudeln mit Käse schmecken mir am besten. Ich habe dieses Gericht bestellt.

Noah
Ich habe Eis mit Kirschen gegessen. Das war ganz lecker!

Felix
Vor dem Hauptgericht hatte ich einen Gurkensalat. Er hat mir sehr gut geschmeckt.

Gabi
Mein Vater isst kein Fleisch. Er hat Kartoffeln mit Salat gegessen.

Leon
Das Tagesgericht war Wiener Schnitzel. Also habe ich das bestellt.

1 0 . 1 Wer hat Fleisch gegessen? **[1 mark]**

1 0 . 2 Wer hat eine Nachspeise gegessen? **[1 mark]**

1 0 . 3 Wer hat sein/ihr Lieblingsessen gegessen? **[1 mark]**

1 0 . 4 Wer hat eine Vorspeise gegessen? **[1 mark]**

1 1 Hunger

Lies die Geschichte aus einem Märchen von den Gebrüdern Grimm über zwei Geschwister.

Beantworte die Fragen.

Schreib **R**, wenn die Aussage **richtig** ist,

F, wenn die Aussage **falsch** ist,

NT, wenn die Aussage **nicht im Text** steht.

> Die Geschwister gingen noch tiefer in den Wald. Es war jetzt der dritte Morgen, dass sie allein im Wald waren. Als es Mittag war, sahen sie einen schneeweißen Vogel. Er sang ein wunderschönes Lied. Die Kinder folgten dem Vogel, bis sie zu einem Häuschen kamen.
>
> Das Haus war aus Brot gebaut und hatte ein Dach aus Kuchen. Die Fenster waren von hellem Zucker. Die Kinder hatten Hunger. Der Junge sagte, „Ich will ein Stück vom Dach essen. Du kannst vom Fenster essen. Das schmeckt süß." Beide Kinder fingen an, ein Stück des Hauses zu essen.
>
> Die Tür ging auf und eine alte Frau kam heraus. Sie nahm die Kinder an der Hand und führte sie ins Haus. Auf dem Tisch war ein gutes Essen: Milch, Pfannkuchen, Äpfel, Nüsse. In der Ecke gab es zwei Betten. Die Kinder legten sich hin und schliefen zufrieden ein.

- The story might appear familiar to you, particularly if it is an extract from a fairy tale, but don't assume that you know the answer without finding it in the text.
- Remember that authentic texts such as stories will often use the imperfect tense, so expect to see multiple examples in a text like this.
- Don't be put off if you don't understand every word. Focus on what the statements say and check these against the text.

▶ Continued

11.1	Die Kinder waren schon seit einer Woche im Wald.		**[1 mark]**
11.2	Der Vogel führte die Kinder zum Haus.		**[1 mark]**
11.3	Es gab Kuchen auf dem Boden.		**[1 mark]**
11.4	Die Kinder haben Teile des Hauses gegessen.		**[1 mark]**
11.5	Die Kinder hatten Angst vor der alten Frau.		**[1 mark]**
11.6	Als sie im Bett waren, waren die Kinder glücklich.		**[1 mark]**

1 2 Technologie

Lies Ralfs Blog.

> Mein Bruder und ich teilen einen altmodischen Computer. Heute muss ich viele E-Mails senden, aber unser Computer funktioniert nicht. Ich will meinen eigenen Computer haben, aber ein neuer Computer kostet zu viel. Meine Eltern haben nicht viel Geld.
>
> Im Arbeitszimmer hat mein Vater einen modernen Laptop. Ich möchte den Laptop benutzen, aber das will mein Vater nicht. Er braucht ihn für seine Arbeit. Mein Vater ist oft schlecht gelaunt, weil er viel Stress hat.

Look out for synonyms, i.e. words or phrases which mean the same as another. An example in this text would be the German for the adjective 'broken', which means the same as 'not working'.

Welche **vier** Aussagen sind **richtig**?

A	Ralf hat seinen eigenen Computer.
B	Ralfs Computer ist nicht sehr modern.
C	Ralfs Computer ist kaputt.
D	Ralf hat heute viele E-Mails geschickt.
E	Ein neuer Computer ist teuer.
F	Ralf darf den Computer seines Vaters benutzen.
G	Ralfs Vater ist arbeitslos.
H	Ralfs Vater ist nicht immer glücklich.

Schreib die **richtigen** Buchstaben in die Kästchen.

[4 marks]

13 Urlaub

Lies die Hotelanzeige.

Beantworte die Fragen auf **Deutsch**.

> **Hotel Zum goldenen Fisch**
>
> Unser gemütliches Hotel am Bodensee ist für alle, die im Urlaub ein bisschen mehr an Luxus wünschen. Wir bieten Ihnen 15 Doppelzimmer mit Dusche, WC und Fernseher. Alle Zimmer haben Balkon oder Terrasse mit Seeblick. Bitte beachten Sie: unser Restaurant ist für zwei Wochen wegen Betriebsferien geschlossen. Zu dieser Zeit lädt Sie unser Partnerhotel *Zum Grünen Frosch* gerne zum Frühstück und Abendessen ein.

> In question 13.1, look carefully at the preposition. Don't be confused between ***vom*** *Zimmer* (from the room) and ***im*** *Zimmer* (in the room) which would get different answers.

13.1 Was kann man vom Zimmer sehen?

_____

[1 mark]

13.2 Warum muss man im Partnerhotel *Zum Grünen Frosch* essen?

_____

[1 mark]

Section C Translation into **English**

1 4 Your Swiss friend has sent you an email.

Translate the email for your friend.

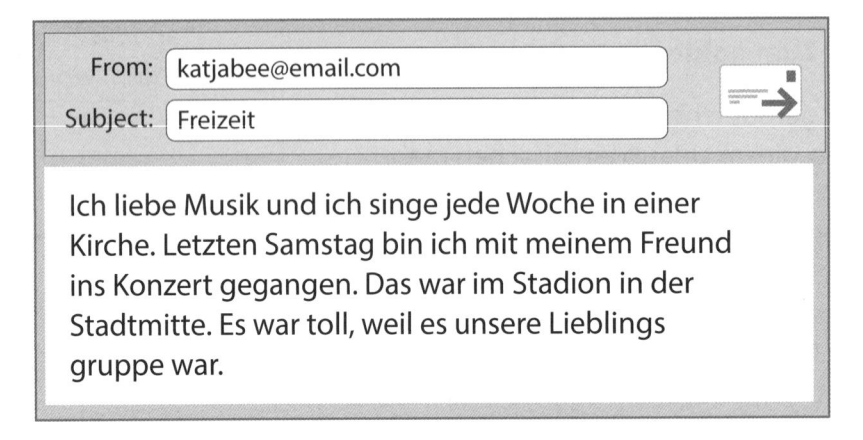

From: katjabee@email.com
Subject: Freizeit

Ich liebe Musik und ich singe jede Woche in einer Kirche. Letzten Samstag bin ich mit meinem Freund ins Konzert gegangen. Das war im Stadion in der Stadtmitte. Es war toll, weil es unsere Lieblingsgruppe war.

[9 marks]

- The first sentence is in the present tense. After that everything is in the past tense. Make sure you use the correct tenses in English.
- Make sure you recognise the difference between singular and plural nouns and translate them correctly.
- Read through your translation when you have finished to check it all makes sense in English.

END OF QUESTIONS

Answers and mark schemes

AQA GCSE German (9-1)

PRACTICE PAPER F

Foundation Tier Paper 4 Writing

Time allowed: 1 hour

Instructions
- You must answer **four** questions.
- You must answer Question 1, Question 2 and Question 3.
- You must answer **either** Question 4.1 **or** Question 4.2. Do not answer both of these questions.
- Answer all questions in **German**.
- Answer the questions in the spaces provided.
- Cross through any work you do not want to be marked.

Information
- The marks for the questions are shown in brackets.
- The maximum mark for this paper is 50.
- You must **not** use a dictionary during this test.
- In order to score the highest marks for Question 4.1/Question 4.2, you must write something about each bullet point. You must use a variety of vocabulary and structures and include your opinions.

Please note: The Practice Paper questions and answers have not been written or approved by AQA.

0 1 Du gehst mit deiner Familie einkaufen und schickst dieses Foto an deinen Freund in der Schweiz.

Schreib **vier** Sätze auf **Deutsch** über das Foto.

0 1 . 1 _____

[2 marks]

0 1 . 2 _____

[2 marks]

0 1 . 3 _____

[2 marks]

0 1 . 4 _____

[2 marks]

- Keep your sentences short and simple. Four or five words are sufficient for each answer.
- If you include too much information you might make a mistake and the mark could be reduced. If you are considering putting two details in one sentence, split it into two separate sentences.
- You must write in full sentences: every sentence must contain a verb to achieve 2 marks.
- It is acceptable to use *Es gibt…* in each sentence, but be aware of word order. If you start the sentence incorrectly with *Gibt es…* you will not gain 2 marks.
- You don't need to talk about what is **not** in the photo, or whether it is in black and white or colour.

0 2 Du schreibst an eine Freundin in Österreich über Technologie.

Schreib etwas über:

- dein Handy
- soziale Medien
- Musik
- Hausaufgaben.

Du musst ungefähr **40** Wörter auf **Deutsch** schreiben.

[16 marks]

- Make sure you cover each bullet point, even if you only write one sentence for one or more of them. Tick them off on the exam paper as you cover each one.
- Don't write too much. Answers which are much longer than 40 words often contain many inaccuracies and the extra words might not be taken into account.
- Although the initial statement tells you that you are writing to a friend, remember that you are writing from **your** point of view. You are not supposed to be the friend in Austria. This statement is just setting the scene for the task so make sure you use *mein* not *dein* when responding to the first bullet point.

0 3 Translate the following sentences into **German**.

I learn history at school.

_____

_____

My friend goes to the cinema at the weekend.

_____

_____

We go home at four o'clock by bus.

_____

_____

The children never eat sweets.

_____

_____

I played music with my family last week.

_____

_____

[10 marks]

- Don't leave any gaps. Have a guess as marks are awarded for communicating the key messages.
- When under pressure, it is easy to write 'I' instead of the pronoun *ich*. Check spellings carefully.
- Learn words which occur frequently in various contexts such as never (*nie*), with (*mit*) and last week (*letzte Woche*).
- In the final sentence you need to use a past tense. Make sure you don't leave out the auxiliary verb (in this case *habe*) or the past participle at the end of the sentence.

Answer **either** Question 4.1 **or** Question 4.2.
You must **not** answer **both** of these questions.

Either Question 4.1

| 0 | 4 | . | 1 | Dein Freund Anton aus der Schweiz hat dich über deine Freunde gefragt. Du schreibst Anton eine E-Mail über deine Freunde.

Schreib:

- etwas über deinen besten Freund/deine beste Freundin
- warum Freunde wichtig sind
- was du in letzter Zeit mit Freunden gemacht hast
- was du nächstes Wochenende mit Freunden machen wirst.

Du musst ungefähr **90** Wörter auf **Deutsch** schreiben.
Schreib etwas über alle Punkte der Aufgabe.

[16 marks]

- You can make up information about a friend for the first bullet point.
- The second bullet point is asking for your opinion. You could use the words *Meiner Meinung nach…* to introduce your opinion.
- The phrase *in letzter Zeit* means 'recently' and indicates that you need to use a past tense.
- It is acceptable to use the present tense when writing about the future, as long as you include future time expressions, such as *nächstes Wochenende*.

Or Question 4.2

| 0 | 4 | . | 2 | Du schreibst ein Blog für eine deutsche Schule über Essen und Trinken bei dir zu Hause.

Schreib:

- etwas über dein Lieblingsessen
- was du nicht gern isst oder trinkst
- was du gestern zum Frühstück gegessen hast
- was du morgen Abend essen wirst.

Du musst ungefähr **90** Wörter auf **Deutsch** schreiben.
Schreib etwas über alle Punkte der Aufgabe.

[16 marks]

- Remember to change *dein* in the question to *mein* in the answer.
- Highlight the word *nicht* in the question to remind you to give a negative opinion.
- Try using words from the bullet points in your answer, e.g. the irregular past participle *gegessen*.
- For the last bullet point, you need to write about something which will happen in the future.
- Make sure you answer the question as given on the exam paper – don't just write a pre-learnt response which might not cover all the bullet points.

END OF QUESTIONS

Model answers and mark schemes

Practice Papers: Set 2

AQA GCSE German (9-1)

F

Foundation Tier Paper 1 Listening

Time allowed: 35 minutes
(including 5 minutes' reading time before the test)

You will need no other materials.
The pauses are pre-recorded for this test.

Information
- The marks for the questions are shown in brackets. The maximum mark for this paper is 40.
- You must **not** use a dictionary.

Advice
This is what you should do for each item.
- After the question number is announced, there will be a pause to allow you to read the instructions and questions.
- Listen carefully to the recording and read the questions again.
- Listen to the recording again, and then answer the questions.
- When the next question is about to start you will hear a bleep.
- You may write at any time during the test.
- In **Section A**, answer the questions in **English**. In **Section B**, answer the questions in **German**.
- You must answer all the questions in the spaces provided. Do not write on blank pages.
- Write neatly and put down all the information you are asked to give.
- **You must not ask questions or interrupt during the test.**
- You have five minutes to read through the question paper. You may make notes during this time. You may turn to the questions now.
- **The test starts now.**

Listen to the audio

Please note: The Practice Paper questions and answers have not been written or approved by AQA.

Section A Questions and answers in **English**

Home town

Mehmet is talking about his home town.

Write the correct letter in the box.

> Listen for the verb 'to visit' (*besuchen*) and focus on the noun that comes straight after it.

0 1 What is there in Mehmet's town?

A   B    C

[1 mark]

0 2 What do tourists visit?

A   B    C

[1 mark]

Practice Papers: Set 2

Social issues

Two callers to a German phone-in programme are giving their opinions.

Answer both parts of the question in **English**.

> The second caller makes one positive and one negative point. Pay careful attention to the wording of question 4.

| 0 | 3 | Which problem does the first caller mention?

_____

[1 mark]

| 0 | 4 | What is the second caller **not** happy with?

_____

[1 mark]

Family

Sven is talking about his family.

Answer the questions in **English**.

> Each part of the question can be answered with a single word. Don't try to write more or you might introduce errors.

| 0 | 5 | Sven and his brother are…

_____

[1 mark]

| 0 | 6 | What is Sven's mother like?

_____

[1 mark]

| 0 | 7 | Which pets would Sven like to have?

_____

[1 mark]

Careers

Jasmin is talking about possible careers.

Write the correct letter in the box.

> The statements here are quite long. Listen to the whole of each statement before making your choice.

0 8 Which advice did Jasmin's careers adviser give her?

A	She should become a teacher.
B	She should choose a job that interests her.
C	She should work with older people.

[1 mark]

0 9 Jasmin does not want to work in a hospital because…

A	the work is poorly paid.
B	the work is hard.
C	the work is uninteresting.

[1 mark]

1 0 Jasmin would like to…

A	travel.
B	work in the open air.
C	earn a lot of money.

[1 mark]

Practice Papers: Set 2

Holidays

Erika is talking about a recent holiday.

Write the correct letter in the box.

> Listen carefully to the verbs: some are in the past tense; others in the present. The questions are all in the past tense, so make sure you listen out for the section of the recording which uses the matching time frame.

1 1 How did Erika's family travel?

A   B   C

[1 mark]

1 2 What was the weather like?

A   B   C

[1 mark]

1 3 Where did they stay?

A   B   C

[1 mark]

Friends

A German boy is talking about some of his friends.

What is each friend like?

A	reliable
B	happy
C	sporty
D	hard-working
E	chatty

Write the correct letter in the box.

> You won't necessarily hear the exact German word for each English adjective in the list. Think about synonyms or other ways of expressing the adjectives. For example, Sofia spends a lot of time on her work so what might that make her?

1 4   Leo   [1 mark]

1 5   Sofia   [1 mark]

1 6   Barbara   [1 mark]

Practice Papers: Set 2

Directions

A pedestrian asks for directions to the animal park.

Answer **both** parts of the question.

Write the correct letter in the box.

> In question 17.1, all three options are mentioned, but which one comes **first**?

1 7 . 1 Which way should she go **first**?

A   B 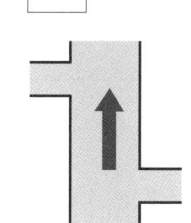   C

[1 mark]

1 7 . 2 Which place is the bus stop in front of?

A   B    C

[1 mark]

Technology

Your Austrian friend Beate is telling you about her use of technology.

Answer the questions in **English**.

> The recording includes several subordinate clauses, in which the verb goes to the end of the sentence. Listen right to the end to understand what is being said.

1 8 How does Beate use her mobile phone?

_____

[1 mark]

1 9 When does Beate find social media useful?

_____

[1 mark]

2 0 Which risk does Beate's mother tell her about?

_____

[1 mark]

Sport

Cleo is talking about different sports.

2 1 Which **three** sports does Cleo do **nowadays**?

A	table tennis
B	hockey
C	skiing
D	swimming
E	cycling
F	basketball

> Listening to the verb tenses and other time clues is essential here. You can rule out any sports that Cleo **used to do** or **would like to do.** Listening for time expressions will help you with this: *Als ich jünger war…, Heute…, Am Wochenende…*, etc.

Write the correct letters in the boxes.

☐ ☐ ☐

[3 marks]

School subjects

An Austrian girl is talking about different school subjects.

What does she think of each subject?

A	fascinating
B	uninteresting
C	hard
D	well taught
E	unimportant

Write the correct letter in the box.

> You won't hear the German for 'well taught', but you can infer this from the description of one of the teachers as patient and helpful.

2 2 science ☐ [1 mark]

2 3 maths ☐ [1 mark]

2 4 history ☐ [1 mark]

Voluntary work

Felix is talking about voluntary work.

Answer both parts of the question in **English**.

> Look carefully at the wording of the questions to help you predict the type of answer you need. To answer question 24.1 you will need a verb, and you'll need to listen out for a noun to answer question 24.2.

2 5 . 1 What did Felix's sister help to do?

_____

[1 mark]

2 5 . 2 Who would Felix like to help when he is older?

_____

[1 mark]

School life

Gudrun is talking about her school life.

Answer **all** parts of the question.

Write the correct letter in the box.

> Small words such as *auch*, *also* and *sogar* can be significant, so listen carefully for the meaning of each sentence.

26.1 What does Gudrun do on school days in the afternoon?

A	She has lessons.
B	She plays sport.
C	She goes home.

[1 mark]

26.2 What is Gudrun's best friend having to do?

A	catch up in the holidays
B	switch to a different school
C	repeat a school year

[1 mark]

26.3 Which school rule does Gudrun **not** like?

A	Mobile phones are banned at break time.
B	Mobile phones can only be used at break time.
C	Mobile phones can be used at break time, but only outside.

[1 mark]

Section B   Questions and answers in **German**

Geburtstag

Karl spricht über seinen Geburtstag.

Beantworte die **beiden** Teile der Frage.

> Revise telling the time in German, especially how to say 'half past'.

27.1 Wann sind Karls Gäste angekommen?

A	B	C
7.30	8.00	8.30

Schreib den richtigen Buchstaben.

[1 mark]

27.2 Welches Geschenk hat Karl von seiner Freundin bekommen?

A   B    C

Schreib den richtigen Buchstaben.

[1 mark]

Wohnorte

Anna spricht über ihren Wohnort.

2 8 Was findet Anna gut an ihrem Wohnort?

A

B

C

D

Schreib die richtigen Buchstaben in die Kästchen.

[2 mark]

Heiraten

Zwei deutsche Freunde sprechen über ihre Pläne für die Zukunft.

Beantworte die Fragen auf **Deutsch**.

- You know from the questions whether each person wants to marry or not, so you just need to listen out for the reasons.
- Remember to answer in German.

2 9 . 1 Warum will Laura **nicht** heiraten?

_____

[1 mark]

2 9 . 2 Warum will Benjamin heiraten?

_____

[1 mark]

Eid al-Fitr

Kathrin spricht über Eid al-Fitr.

30 Wie hat ihre Familie Eid al-Fitr **letztes Jahr** gefeiert?

> Verb tenses and negatives are key to identifying the correct answer options here. Listen carefully to the whole extract before selecting the answers.

A	Sie haben das Haus mit Lichtern dekoriert.
B	Sie sind in die Moschee gegangen.
C	Sie haben ihre Hände mit Henna dekoriert.
D	Die Oma ist zu Besuch gekommen.

Schreib die richtigen Buchstaben in die Kästchen.

[2 marks]

END OF QUESTIONS

Answers and mark schemes

AQA GCSE German (9-1)

PRACTICE PAPER F

Practice Papers: Set 2

Foundation Tier Paper 2 Speaking

Time allowed: 7–9 minutes
(+12 minutes' supervised preparation time)

Candidate's material – Role-play and Photo card

Instructions
- During the preparation time you must prepare the Role-play card and Photo card stimulus cards given to you.
- You may make notes during the preparation time on the paper provided by your teacher-examiner. Do not write on the stimulus cards.
- Hand your notes and both stimulus cards to the teacher-examiner before the General Conversation.
- You must ask the teacher-examiner at least one question in the General Conversation.

Information
- The test will last a maximum of 9 minutes and will consist of a Role-play (approximately 2 minutes) and a Photo card (approximately 2 minutes), followed by a General Conversation (3–5 minutes) based on your nominated Theme and the remaining Theme which has not been covered in the Photo card.
- You must **not** use a dictionary at any time during the test. This includes the preparation time.

Teacher's scripts

Please note: The Practice Paper questions and answers have not been written or approved by AQA.

Practice Papers: Set 2

ROLE-PLAY 1

CANDIDATE'S ROLE

Part 1

Instructions to candidates

Your teacher will play the part of your German friend and will speak first.

You should address your friend as *du*.

When you see this – **!** – you will have to respond to something you have not prepared.

When you see this – **?** – you will have to ask a question.

Du sprichst mit deinem Freund / deiner Freundin aus Deutschland über Musik.

- **?** Konzerte.
- Musikfestival hier – wann.
- **!**
- Musik hören – wo (**zwei** Details).
- Musiksendungen – deine Meinung.

- A variety of question words is used in this role-play. Make sure you revise all your question words and try not to mix them up.
- For the first bullet point, think of an appropriate question to ask about concerts. A yes/no question might be easiest, such as 'Do you go to concerts?'.
- For the second bullet point, assume that there is going to be a music festival in your town. Say when it takes place, but avoid using the verb *stattfinden* unless you are really confident.
- In preparation for the unexpected question, think of a general question about music that a friend who does not know you well might ask.
- Mention two different places for the fourth bullet point and join them with *und* or *oder*. You will need to use the dative case after *in*.
- A simple opinion is fine for the last bullet point. If you use *gern*, don't forget the verb.

ROLE-PLAY 2

CANDIDATE'S ROLE

Part 1

Instructions to candidates

Your teacher will play the part of the receptionist and will speak first.

You should address the receptionist as *Sie*.

When you see this – **!** – you will have to respond to something you have not prepared.

When you see this – **?** – you will have to ask a question.

Sie sprechen mit dem Rezeptionisten / der Rezeptionistin in einem Hotel in Österreich.

- Reservierung – wie viele Nächte.
- **!**
- Im Hotel essen (**ein** Detail).
- Besuch – warum.
- **?** Preis der Übernachtung.

- Expect the teacher-examiner to use the formal *Sie* form in this role-play and be ready to use it yourself if necessary.
- You can just say 'I have a booking…' for the first bullet point without the need to use a verb meaning 'to stay'. Be careful with pronunciation as it could affect meaning or understanding: for example, *für* can sometimes be mistakenly pronounced as *vor*.
- For the second bullet point, what might a hotel receptionist ask you in order to find your booking on the system?
- Mention at least one meal for the third response that you know how to say in German.
- Think of a plausible and straightforward reason for your visit to answer the fourth question, e.g. visiting friends, a holiday or a sports event.
- In a real situation you would probably ask for confirmation of a price you had already seen. But don't make things complicated here – simply ask how much the stay costs.

ROLE-PLAY 3

CANDIDATE'S ROLE

Part 1

Instructions to candidates

Your teacher will play the part of your Swiss friend and will speak first.

You should address your friend as *du*.

When you see this – **!** – you will have to respond to something you have not prepared.

When you see this – **?** – you will have to ask a question.

Du sprichst mit deinem Freund / deiner Freundin aus der Schweiz über das Leben nach der Schule.

- Schule verlassen – wann.
- Uni – warum oder warum nicht.
- Was für Arbeit (**zwei** Details).
- **!**
- **?** Berufserfahrung.

- Rather than giving a date for the first bullet point, it is probably easier to say 'in two years' time' or similar. Remember that *in* takes the dative case in time phrases.
- Think of one simple reason why you want – or don't want – to go to university. Make sure your answer to the next question follows on logically.
- Since two details are required in response to the third bullet point, you could mention a general area such as working outdoors and then a specific job.
- Think about which question word the teacher-examiner might use for the unexpected question. You have already answered questions beginning with *wann*, *warum* and *was*.
- Your question about work experience can be in any tense and doesn't have to relate to your Swiss friend, e.g. it could be 'Is work experience good?'.

Card A Candidate's Photo card

Part 2

- Look at the photo during the preparation period.
- Make any notes you wish to on an additional piece of paper.
- Your teacher will then ask you questions about the photo and about topics related to **technology in everyday life**.

Your teacher will ask you the following three questions and then **two more questions** which you have not prepared.

- Was gibt es auf dem Foto?
- Was für Technologien benutzt du zu Hause?
- Wie hast du letzte Woche neue Technologien benutzt?

> - For the first question, you could mention the three types of device in the photograph. You could also say who and where the people are – presumably a family in their living room.
> - Try not to repeat the vocabulary you used to answer the first question in response to the second question. To extend your answer you could say what you use technology for, e.g. chatting to friends, taking photos.
> - Try to give a range of activities in your third answer; this will enable you to use various perfect tense verbs such as *Ich habe ... gesurft/ geschickt/telefoniert/herunterladen*, etc.
> - For the unexpected questions, think of aspects of the topic that have not been covered so far in this photo card task, such as the disadvantages and dangers of technology or which type of technology you consider to be the best.

Card B   **Candidate's Photo card**

Part 2

- Look at the photo during the preparation period.
- Make any notes you wish to on an additional piece of paper.
- Your teacher will then ask you questions about the photo and about topics related to **travel and tourism.**

Your teacher will ask you the following three questions and then **two more questions** which you have not prepared.

- Was gibt es auf dem Foto?
- Schläfst du gern in einem Zelt? … Warum (nicht)?
- Was hast du letztes Jahr im Urlaub gemacht?

> - In response to the first question, you can say who the people are, where they are located and what they are doing. You might also comment on the weather.
> - For question 2, think of at least one advantage or disadvantage of camping. You could develop your answer either by talking about a different type of accommodation or by giving a further opinion about camping, such as a past experience.
> - In talking about past holiday experiences in question 3, you could talk about a country or place you visited, activities you did whilst on holiday, the weather and your opinion of the holiday.
> - Prepare to answer questions on different holiday destinations and different types of holiday activities for the unexpected questions.

Card C   **Candidate's Photo card**

Part 2

- Look at the photo during the preparation period.
- Make any notes you wish to on an additional piece of paper.
- Your teacher will then ask you questions about the photo and about topics related to **jobs, career choices and ambitions**.

Your teacher will ask you the following three questions and then **two more questions** which you have not prepared.

- Was gibt es auf dem Foto?
- Wie findest du Gartenarbeit?
- Wo möchtest du später arbeiten? … Warum?

> - For question 1, a brief description of the man would be appropriate, plus some reference to the work he is doing. You could also mention what you see in the background of the picture (*Im Hintergrund sieht man…*).
> - For the second question, try to use at least one adjective other than *gut*. You could compare gardening with a different job and say which option you would prefer.
> - The answer to *wo* in question 3 could be a country, a specific place such as your home town or a type of workplace.
> - Expect a question about preparation for the world of work, which could involve work experience or studying at university. You could also be asked about the jobs or job aspirations of other people, such as parents and friends.
> - Pay attention to the person of the question so you respond correctly. For example, if you are being asked a question about a friend's plans for the future, you will need to use the third person (*er/sie*) rather than the first person (*ich*).

GENERAL CONVERSATION

Part 3

The Photo card is followed by a General Conversation. The first part of the conversation will be on a theme nominated by the candidate and the second part on the other theme not covered by the Photo card. The total time for the General Conversation will be between **three and five minutes** and a similar amount of time should be spent on each theme. Here is a reminder of the three themes:

- Identity and culture
- Local, national, international and global areas of interest
- Current and future study and employment

The following pages show two examples of the general conversation with accompanying commentary on how these conversations would be marked, followed by tasks.

Conversation 1: Themes 2 and 3

Wir beginnen mit Thema 2. Beschreib dein Haus oder deine Wohnung.
Mein Haus ist klein und modern.

Magst du dein Haus?
Ja, ich finde es toll.

Und wie ist dein Zimmer?
Es ist toll.

Wo möchtest du in der Zukunft wohnen?
In der Schweiz.

Warum?
Ich habe Freunde dort.

Was machst du zu Hause für die Umwelt?
Ich trenne den Müll.

Wie oft?
Jeden Tag.

Was recycelst du?
Altglas und Dosen.

Gibt es Umweltprobleme in deinem Wohnort?
Ja.

Was für Umweltprobleme?
Zu viele Autos. Wir brauchen mehr Busse.

Hast du eine Frage für mich?
Wie ist Ihr Wohnort?

Meine Stadt ist schön. Und jetzt machen wir Thema 3. Wie groß ist deine Schule?
Sie ist groß.

Wie viele Schüler und Schülerinnen hat sie?
Mehr als zweitausend.

Was hast du gestern in der Schule gelernt?
Deutsch, Englisch und Mathe.

Was ist dein Lieblingsfach?
Mathe.

Warum?
Ich verstehe alles.

Beschreib einen typischen Schultag.
Die Schule beginnt um Viertel vor neun. Wir haben fünf Stunden pro Tag.

Willst du später auf die Uni gehen?
Ja.

Was möchtest du studieren?
Mathe.

Wo möchtest du später arbeiten?
Im Ausland.

Marks and commentary

	Communication	Range and accuracy of language	Pronunciation and intonation	Spontaneity and fluency	Total
Marks	5/10	6/10	3/5	3/5	**17/30**

The conversation has been awarded 5 marks for Communication, as only short responses are given, a number of which do not include a verb. The responses could be developed by answering in full sentences, adapting the questions in order to formulate the answers. Opinions are successfully conveyed when they are talking about their house and bedroom, but could be backed up with reasons in order to gain higher marks. An appropriate question is asked of the teacher-examiner, correctly using the polite form of the possessive adjective, but the teacher-examiner has to prompt it.

A mark of 6 has been awarded for Range and accuracy of language because basic language with simple structures is used, such as present tense verbs. There are no successful references to past or future time frames. Although the teacher-examiner asks questions about the past and future, the responses do not include verbs and therefore cannot be credited as examples of different time frames.

It is assumed that the pronunciation is largely intelligible but with little attempt at intonation. There may be difficulties with umlauts and vowels, such as the *ä* in *später*, and with the *i* in *finde*.

It is assumed that there are frequent hesitations and that delivery is generally slow. A few responses may be more fluent but the lack of intonation suggests that they have been pre-learnt. This results in a mark of 3 for Spontaneity and fluency.

1. **Try to give more detail by inserting an appropriate qualifier or adverb (meaning, for example, 'very', 'fairly', 'always', 'often') into each of the following phrases:**

   a) *Mein Haus ist … klein.*
   b) *Ich trenne … den Müll.*
   c) *Sie [Die Schule] ist … groß.*
   d) *… im Ausland.* (try 'perhaps' here)

2. **How could you extend the responses without verbs in the second part of the conversation (from *Wie groß ist deine Schule?*). For example, instead of just saying *Mathe*, you could say *Ich werde (bestimmt) Mathe studieren*. Try to form your answers without repeating the exact words of the question, ideally.**

Conversation 2: Themes 2 and 3

Wir beginnen mit Thema 2. Beschreib dein Haus oder deine Wohnung.
Mein Haus ist ziemlich groß und sehr modern. Wir haben eine Küche, ein Wohnzimmer und drei Schlafzimmer im ersten Stock.

Magst du dein Haus?
Ja, ich finde es toll. Ich habe mein eigenes Zimmer und es ist bequem.

Wo möchtest du in der Zukunft wohnen?
Ich möchte in der Schweiz wohnen. Ich habe Familie und Freunde dort. Ich fahre auch gern Ski.

Was machst du zu Hause für die Umwelt?
Ich trenne jeden Tag den Müll. Ich recycle Altglas, Altpapier und Dosen. Ich mache das Licht aus, bevor ich ausgehe.

Sparst du auch Wasser?
Ja. Ich dusche, anstatt zu baden. Das spart viel Wasser.

Gibt es Umweltprobleme in deinem Wohnort?
Ja. Es gibt zu viele Autos. Sie machen Lärm und verschmutzen die Luft. Wir brauchen bessere öffentliche Verkehrsmittel und mehr Fußgängerzonen.

Sieht man auch Leute, die keine Wohnung haben?
Ja, man sieht arme Leute auf der Straße. Sie müssen betteln, um zu überleben. Das ist traurig. Mögen Sie Ihren Wohnort?

Ja, meine Stadt ist schön. Und jetzt machen wir Thema 3. Wie groß ist deine Schule?
Sie ist sehr groß. Es gibt mehr als zweitausend Schüler und Schülerinnen, aber wir haben keine Oberstufe.

Was hast du gestern in der Schule gemacht?
Ich habe Deutsch, Englisch und Mathe gelernt. Am Nachmittag habe ich Tennis gespielt.

Und in der Pause?
Ich habe zu Mittag gegessen. Dann habe ich mit meinen Freunden geplaudert. Das Wetter war schlecht und wir sind im Klassenzimmer geblieben.

Was ist dein Lieblingsfach?
Ich lerne am liebsten Mathe. Die Lehrerin ist immer geduldig und ich verstehe alles.

Beschreib einen typischen Schultag.
Die Schule beginnt um Viertel vor neun. Wir haben fünf Stunden pro Tag. Wir gehen um halb vier nach Hause.

Willst du später auf die Uni gehen?
Ja, ich möchte Mathe studieren. Zuerst muss ich aber gute Noten in den Prüfungen bekommen.

Welchen Beruf willst du machen?
Ich möchte im Ausland arbeiten, vielleicht mit Computern. Ich finde Informatik interessant.

Marks and commentary

	Communication	Range and accuracy of language	Pronunciation and intonation	Spontaneity and fluency	Total
Marks	10/10	10/10	5/5	5/5	**30/30**

The conversation scores full marks for Communication: extended responses are given where it is appropriate to do so, for example, when talking about the school, an additional comment is made about the lack of a Sixth Form. Information and opinions are conveyed clearly and some opinions are explained. For example, it is explained why maths is the favourite subject. An appropriate question is asked of the teacher-examiner spontaneously without the need to be prompted, and the polite form of the verb is used correctly.

The full 10 marks have been awarded for Range and accuracy of language because a good variety of linguistic structures is used, with no unnecessary repetition. There are some examples of complex language, such as *bevor ich ausgehe, um zu überleben* and several modal verbs followed by an infinitive. The future is referred to successfully when talking about where they would like to live, what they would like to study and which job they would like to do, and to the past when talking about what they did in school yesterday.

It is assumed that the pronunciation and intonation are generally good but with some inconsistency at times. Minor errors might include the vowel in *Lärm* and the *ch* in *Nachmittag*.

It is assumed that a suitable pace is maintained, but some hesitations are made, especially in longer responses. Despite the hesitations, the conversation would still gain 5 marks for Spontaneity and fluency.

1. **Several adverbs of time and frequency are used such as:** *jeden Tag, immer, zuerst, am Nachmittag and dann*. **Try to find other responses in which you could add further adverbs of time and frequency such as** *oft, selten, um ... Uhr, jede Woche*.

2. **Focus on the opportunities within the conversation where it is possible to use past and future time frames. See if you can extend some of the answers by making a comment in the past or future. For example, in response to the first question about school, you could say that you will go to a different school or college for the sixth form**.

Model answers and mark schemes

Practice Papers: Set 2

AQA GCSE German (9-1)

F

Foundation Tier Paper 3 Reading

Time allowed: 45 minutes

Instructions
- Answer **all** questions.
- Answer the questions in the spaces provided.
- In **Section A**, answer the questions in **English**. In **Section B**, answer the questions in **German**. In **Section C**, translate the passage into **English**.
- Cross through any work you do not want to be marked.

Information
- The marks for the questions are shown in brackets.
- The maximum mark for this paper is 60.
- You must **not** use a dictionary.

Please note: The Practice Paper questions and answers have not been written or approved by AQA.

Section A   Questions and answers in **English**

0 1   **Family**

Philipp's father has sent him a text message.

Answer the questions in **English**.

> Heute Abend kommt dein Onkel auf Besuch. Ich muss zu Hause aufräumen. Ich habe keine Zeit, um einkaufen zu gehen. Geh bitte zum Lebensmittelgeschäft und kaufe Brot, Schinken und Eier. Danke. Komm nicht zu spät nach Hause.

0 1 . 1   When is Philipp's uncle arriving?

[1 mark]

▶ Continued

0 1 . 2 Why will Philipp's father not have any time to go shopping?

_____

[1 mark]

0 1 . 3 Apart from bread, name **one** thing Philipp has to buy.

_____

[1 mark]

0 2 **Post-16 plans**

Read the contributions by four teenagers on an online forum about future plans.

Write the first letter of the correct name in the box.

Write **T** for Tamara.
Write **W** for Wilhelm.
Write **M** for Margit.
Write **E** for Elise.

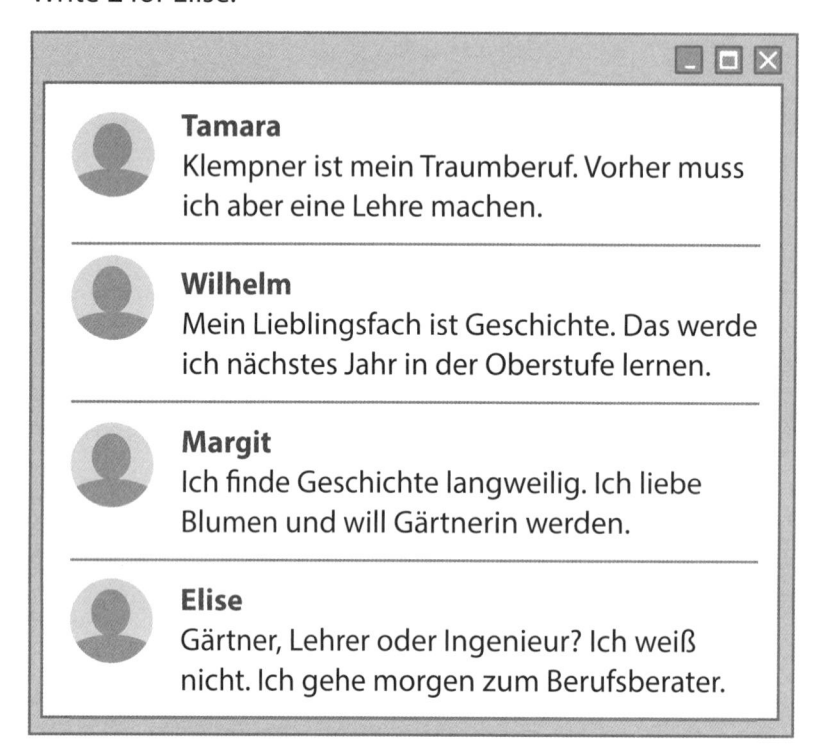

Tamara
Klempner ist mein Traumberuf. Vorher muss ich aber eine Lehre machen.

Wilhelm
Mein Lieblingsfach ist Geschichte. Das werde ich nächstes Jahr in der Oberstufe lernen.

Margit
Ich finde Geschichte langweilig. Ich liebe Blumen und will Gärtnerin werden.

Elise
Gärtner, Lehrer oder Ingenieur? Ich weiß nicht. Ich gehe morgen zum Berufsberater.

0 2 . 1 Whose future plans show an interest in nature? [1 mark]

0 2 . 2 Who is planning to go into Sixth Form? [1 mark]

0 2 . 3 Who needs advice about his/her future? [1 mark]

0 2 . 4 Who has to do an apprenticeship first? [1 mark]

03 "Der Biberpelz", a play by Gerhart Hauptmann

Read these stage directions from the play.

> Morgens gegen acht Uhr in der Wohnung der Frau Wolff. Auf dem Herd kocht das Kaffeewasser. Frau Wolff sitzt auf einem Stuhl und zählt Geld. Julius kommt herein. Er trägt ein totes Kaninchen.

Write the correct letter in the box.

03.1 The scene is set…

A	early in the day.
B	in the middle of the day.
C	towards the end of the day.

[1 mark]

03.2 On stage there is…

A	a table.
B	a cooker.
C	a wardrobe.

[1 mark]

03.3 Frau Wolff is…

A	drinking coffee.
B	counting money.
C	cooking a meal.

[1 mark]

03.4 Julius is carrying…

A	a rabbit.
B	a guinea pig.
C	a bird.

[1 mark]

0 4 **Home and family**

Read Mark's email to his new German friend.

Answer the questions in **English**.

> Von: mark@email.com
> Betreff: Hallo
>
> Hallo
>
> Wie geht's? Meine Familie und ich wohnen in einem Reihenhaus in einem Dorf. Meine Eltern kommen gut mit unserer Nachbarin aus. Sie ist sehr freundlich. Donnerstags gehe ich nach der Schule mit meiner Schwester zu ihrem Haus, weil meine Mutter spät arbeitet. Dort machen wir unsere Hausaufgaben und sehen ein bisschen fern. Die Nachbarin ist sehr nett und gibt uns immer ein Glas Orangensaft und ein paar Kekse.
>
> Dein Mark

It is a good idea to highlight or underline the question word (i.e. 'where', 'why' and 'what' in these questions) and then ensure that your answer corresponds to it. For example, if the question is '**Where**…?', the answer can't be 'on Thursdays'.

0 4 . 1 Where does Mark's family live? Give **two** details.

_____

_____

[2 marks]

0 4 . 2 Where does Mark go once a week after school?

_____

[1 mark]

0 4 . 3 Why does he have to go there?

_____

[1 mark]

0 4 . 4 What does he eat there?

_____

[1 mark]

0 5 **Mobile phones**

A Swiss school has published a pupil survey about how mobile phones are used. Read the results.

56% der Schüler sind Mädchen.
44% der Schüler sind Jungen.
90% surfen jeden Abend im Internet.
78% lesen regelmäßig E-Mails.
83% schicken täglich Kurznachrichten.
37% machen Einkäufe online.
50% laden neue Lieder herunter.
62% benutzen es für Spiele.

> In many tasks you will find the answers in the order in which they appear in the text. This sort of question is different. The answers can appear in any order, so read each statement in the text carefully.

Write the correct **number** in each box.

0 5 . 1 What percentage of pupils are girls? [1 mark]

0 5 . 2 What percentage of pupils download music? [1 mark]

0 5 . 3 What percentage of pupils regularly send texts? [1 mark]

0 5 . 4 What percentage of pupils shop online? [1 mark]

06 A typical day

You read a blog post by Jana about a typical day in the school holidays.

> Ich stehe etwas später auf, normalerweise gegen zehn Uhr. Meine Eltern und mein Bruder stehen schon um acht Uhr auf. Deshalb frühstücke ich allein.
>
> Ich treibe gern Sport und ich gehe jeden Nachmittag ins Fitnessstudio. Vor dem Mittagessen gehe ich aber ins Hallenbad.
>
> Mein Vater und ich interessieren uns für Motorsport. Manchmal kauft er eine Zeitschrift über Autos, und ich lese sie gern.
>
> Am Abend sehen wir fern, aber mein Bruder und ich streiten uns immer. Ich will eine Sportsendung sehen. Er sieht lieber Seifenopern.

Complete the sentences in **English**.

06.1 Jana usually gets up at around…

[1 mark]

06.2 Jana eats breakfast…

[1 mark]

06.3 In the morning she goes to the…

[1 mark]

06.4 Her father often buys…

[1 mark]

06.5 On TV, her brother likes watching…

[1 mark]

07 Travel and tourism

Read the conversation in a German chat room between three teenagers who are exchanging views on holidays.

Write the **four** correct holiday activities in the grid.

> Pay attention to time expressions such as *nächstes Jahr, dieses Jahr* and *früher*, as these are indications of the past, present or future tense.

Frederik
Meine Eltern müssen diesen Sommer arbeiten, also bleiben wir zu Hause. Nächstes Jahr will ich unbedingt ins Ausland reisen. Zelten mag ich überhaupt nicht, weil das Wetter oft schlecht ist. Unser letzter Familienurlaub war in einem Wohnwagen.

Silke
Das Reiseziel für meinen Traumurlaub ist irgendwo in Griechenland, und ich habe vor, irgendwann dorthin zu fahren. Ich liege so gern am Strand. Früher sind wir in den Sommerferien oft in den Bergen gewandert. Dieses Jahr sind wir in Rom, um die Sehenswürdigkeiten zu besichtigen.

Alex
In Zukunft will ich auch Urlaub am Strand machen. Mein Freund und ich sind begeisterte Radler. Letztes Jahr waren wir an der Ostsee. Diesen Sommer machen wir eine 1-wöchige Tour am Radweg entlang der Donau.

	Past	Present	Future
Frederik		staying at home	
Silke	went hiking in the mountains	sightseeing in Rome	
Alex	was with friend at the Baltic Sea		beach holiday

[4 marks]

0 8 School

Read this case study from a website aimed at parents of teenagers.

> Florian geht auf eine Ganztagsschule. Sein Freund Hannes geht auf eine andere Schule. Sie treffen sich am Abend oder am Wochenende. Die Freunde hören gern Musik und spielen Schach zusammen.
>
> Florian mag nicht alle Fächer in der Schule. Im Zeugnis bekommt er eine Zwei in Mathe. Er bekommt eine Fünf in Biologie und in Spanisch hat er die gleiche Note. Es ist möglich, dass er sitzen bleibt. Seine Eltern machen sich keine Sorgen. Sie wissen, dass Florian fleißig ist.

Which **four** statements are true?

A	Florian and Hannes often meet up in the afternoon.
B	They like playing squash and listening to music together.
C	Their hobbies are listening to music and playing chess.
D	Florian only likes some subjects at school.
E	Florian is quite good at maths.
F	Florian is better at Spanish than biology.
G	Florian has already had to repeat a year.
H	Florian's parents are not concerned about him.

Write the correct letters in the boxes.

[4 marks]

Section B Questions and answers in **German**

0 9 **Umwelt**

Lies Inges Blog.

Beantworte die Fragen.

Schreib **R**, wenn die Aussage **richtig** ist,

F, wenn die Aussage **falsch** ist,

NT, wenn die Aussage **nicht im Text** steht.

> In meiner Stadt gibt es zu viel Verkehr. Man sollte neue Fahrradwege statt Straßen bauen. Benzin ist teuer, aber Radfahren ist fast kostenlos und auch gesund. Unsere Stadtmitte ist nicht so verschmutzt wie einige Städte im Ausland, aber die Luft ist trotzdem nicht sauber. Ich fahre am liebsten mit der Bahn, aber das ist leider nicht immer möglich.

> Look carefully for words used in the text and in the statements which either mean exactly the same thing, or which mean the opposite. For example, in question 9.2, the word *billig* (cheap) is used. You could be looking in the text for another word which means that something doesn't cost very much, or you could be looking for the word for expensive (*teuer*), perhaps used with a negative. Which is it?

0 9 . 1 Man sollte Straßen bauen. **[1 mark]**

0 9 . 2 Radfahren ist billig. **[1 mark]**

0 9 . 3 Die Luftqualität ist schlecht. **[1 mark]**

0 9 . 4 Es gibt keinen Bahnhof in Inges Stadt. **[1 mark]**

1 0 Feste

Ergänze den Text mit einem Wort von der Liste unten.

A	Kirche
B	Maifeiertag
C	Nikolaus
D	Ostereier
E	Umzug
F	Weihnachtsbaum

Schreib den richtigen Buchstaben in das Kästchen.

1 0 . 1 Es ist Heiliger Abend. Wir werden heute den ☐ schmücken. **[1 mark]**

1 0 . 2 Jetzt ist wieder Karneval. Es gibt einen großen ☐ durch die Stadt. **[1 mark]**

1 0 . 3 Heute ist Karfreitag. Am Sonntag werden wir ☐ suchen. **[1 mark]**

11 In den Alpen

Lies diese Geschichte aus dem Buch „Heidi", geschrieben von Johanna Spyri.

Beantworte die Fragen auf **Deutsch**.

Vom Dorf Maienfeld führt ein Fußweg durch grüne Bäume zu den Alpen hinauf. Am hellen, sonnigen Junimorgen ging eine große, kräftige Frau auf diesem schmalen Fußweg. Sie führte ein Kind an der Hand. Trotz der heißen Sonne trug das Kind warme Winterkleidung. Es setzte sich auf den Boden.

„Bist du müde, Heidi?", fragte die Frau.

„Nein, es ist mir heiß", antwortete das Kind.

„Wir müssen nur noch eine Stunde gehen, bis wir oben sind. Dann bleibst du beim Alten. Er ist dein Großvater und muss für dich sorgen."

Der Alte, der allein in einer Hütte in den Bergen wohnte, hatte dicke Augenbrauen und einen grauen Bart. Er war manchmal unfreundlich.

- You must answer this question in German. Any answers in English will be ignored and will gain no marks.
- Look carefully for the correct number and type of details for each question. For question 11.1, you need to find two reasons that might not be obviously given as reasons in the text. In question 11.2, make sure you focus on appearance and don't be distracted by additional details such as personality traits or where the grandfather lives.

11.1 Warum sagte Heidi, „Es ist mir heiß"? Gib **zwei** Details.

_____

_____

[2 marks]

11.2 Wie sah Heidis Großvater aus? Gib **zwei** Details.

_____

_____

[2 marks]

12 Feiern

Lies die Online-Diskussion über Feiern.

Schreib den richtigen Buchstaben in das Kästchen.

Schreib **A** für Andrea.
Schreib **T** für Theo.
Schreib **F** für Florian.
Schreib **W** für Werner.

Andrea
Meine Schwester wird im Juli heiraten. Ich freue mich schon darauf. Ich habe ein neues Kleid aus grüner Seide.

Theo
Meine Mutter hat morgen Geburtstag. Ich habe Blumen für sie gekauft. Mein Vater backt einen großen Geburtstagskuchen, weil unsere Familie groß ist.

Florian
Mein Bruder hat sich endlich verlobt. Die ganze Familie geht zusammen essen, um seine Verlobung zu feiern.

Werner
Meine Großeltern sind seit vierzig Jahren verheiratet. Sie haben uns eingeladen, mit ihnen eine Woche am Mittelmeer zu verbringen.

12.1 Wer geht ins Restaurant? **[1 mark]**

12.2 Wer geht zu einer Hochzeit? **[1 mark]**

12.3 Wer geht auf eine Reise? **[1 mark]**

1 3 Skispringen

Lies die Webseite über Skispringen.

Norbert Schäfer, vierzehn Jahre alt, ist ein Star der Zukunft im Skispringen. Er freut sich schon auf die kommenden Juniorenmeisterschaften in der Schweiz. Der Schüler aus der österreichischen Kleinstadt Landeck hat noch keinen ersten Platz gewonnen. Aber er hofft, dass sich diese Situation dieses Jahr ändern wird.

Norbert hat einen Ausbildungsplatz an einem Skigymnasium. Das ist ein Internat für Jugendliche zwischen 14 und 20 Jahren. Dort steht man früh auf: Die erste Stunde gibt es schon vor dem Frühstück. Am Vormittag gibt es Unterricht, auch an Samstagen, und das Training findet am Nachmittag statt.

Das Training ist hart und ermüdend, aber das macht Norbert nichts aus. Er ist dankbar, dass er einen der wenigen Ausbildungsplätze an dieser Schule bekommen hat. Viele Wintersportler, die später bei den Olympischen Spielen Erfolg hatten, haben hier angefangen.

> Look closely at every word in the statements, rather than being satisfied with the gist of what they mean. It is easy to attach too little importance to words like *zu* in statement F, or *viele* in statement G. If you removed both of these words, the statements would have a slightly different emphasis.

Welche **vier** Aussagen sind **richtig**?

A	Norbert kommt aus Österreich.
B	Norbert hat den ersten Platz in den Juniorenmeisterschaften gewonnen.
C	Norbert schläft an seiner Schule.
D	An seiner Schule hat man jeden Tag Unterricht.
E	Nach dem Mittagessen geht er nicht ins Klassenzimmer.
F	Norbert findet das Training zu ermüdend.
G	Es gibt viele Plätze für begabte Jugendliche an dieser Schule.
H	Norbert freut sich, dass er diese Schule besucht.

Schreib die **richtigen** Buchstaben in die Kästchen.

[4 marks]

Section C Translation into **English**

1 4 Your German friend has sent you an email.

Translate the email.

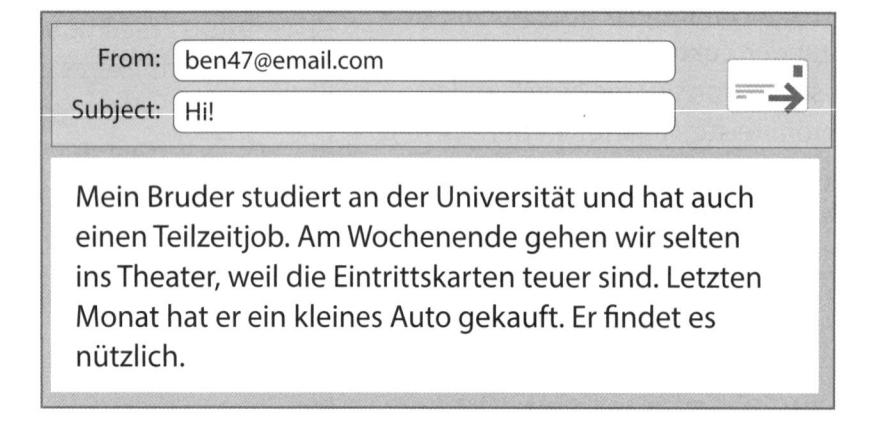

From: ben47@email.com
Subject: Hi!

Mein Bruder studiert an der Universität und hat auch einen Teilzeitjob. Am Wochenende gehen wir selten ins Theater, weil die Eintrittskarten teuer sind. Letzten Monat hat er ein kleines Auto gekauft. Er findet es nützlich.

[9 marks]

- Don't leave any gaps in your translation. If you don't know a word, have a guess as the words you do know won't gain any marks if they don't form part of a coherent sentence.
- Pay attention to 'small' words such as *auch* and *selten*. If you miss them out, you won't gain the mark.

END OF QUESTIONS

Answers and mark schemes

Practice Papers: Set 2

AQA GCSE German (9-1)

PRACTICE PAPER

F

Foundation Tier Paper 4 Writing

Time allowed: 1 hour

Instructions
- You must answer **four** questions.
- You must answer Question 1, Question 2 and Question 3.
- You must answer **either** Question 4.1 **or** Question 4.2. Do not answer both of these questions.
- Answer all questions in **German**.
- Answer the questions in the spaces provided.
- Cross through any work you do not want to be marked.

Information
- The marks for the questions are shown in brackets.
- The maximum mark for this paper is 50.
- You must **not** use a dictionary during this test.
- In order to score the highest marks for Question 4.1/Question 4.2, you must write something about each bullet point. You must use a variety of vocabulary and structures and include your opinions.

Please note: The Practice Paper questions and answers have not been written or approved by AQA.

0 1 Du bist mit Freunden und schickst dieses Foto an deine Freundin in Österreich.

Schreib **vier** Sätze auf **Deutsch** über das Foto.

0 1 . 1

_____

[2 marks]

0 1 . 2

_____

[2 marks]

0 1 . 3

_____

[2 marks]

0 1 . 4

_____

[2 marks]

- Don't repeat the same information using different words in a separate sentence. For example, *Es gibt fünf Teenager auf einem Sofa* has the same meaning as *Fünf Teenager sind auf einem Sofa*. If you write both of these, you will only be awarded one set of 2 marks.
- Use the present tense correctly in German. Remember that the German for 'they are sitting' is the same as for 'they sit': *sie sitzen*.
- If you don't know the German word for something, avoid simply writing the English. Instead, choose something else to say.
- Spelling is important so try to be as accurate as possible.

0 2 Du schreibst an einen Freund in der Schweiz über gesundes Leben.

Schreib etwas über:

- gesundes Essen
- Sport
- Alkohol
- Drogen.

Du musst ungefähr **40** Wörter auf **Deutsch** schreiben.

[16 marks]

> - Avoid repeating the same sentence structure for each bullet point. For example, if you write *Ich mag…* at the start of each sentence, it will seem repetitive and you will get a lower mark than if you varied your sentences.
> - Make sure each sentence contains a verb, such as *Ich **trinke**…* or *Sport **ist**…*
> - Add interest by including qualifiers such as *sehr* (very) or *ziemlich* (fairly).
> - You could say how often you take part in activities by using the adverbs *immer* (always), *oft* (often) or *nie* (never).

0 3 Translate the following sentences into **German**.

I have a brother and a sister.

_____

_____

My parents like living in the town centre.

_____

_____

The teacher travels to school by car.

_____

_____

We must buy cheese today.

_____

_____

I did the homework with my friend.

_____

_____

[10 marks]

- Take care with present tense endings. You need to use verbs in the first person singular (*ich;* ending -*e*) and third person singular (*der Lehrer;* ending -*t*) here, as well as the first and third person plural (*wir/meine Eltern;* ending -*en*). There are up to 5 marks given for application of grammatical structures, so it is essential to learn verb endings.
- If you are using *gern* in the second sentence to express the sense of 'like', remember that it is not a verb. It must be used along with a verb, in this case 'live'.

Answer **either** Question 4.1 **or** Question 4.2.
You must **not** answer **both** of these questions.

Either Question 4.1

0 4 . 1   Du schreibst eine E-Mail an deine Freundin Anna über dein Haus.

Schreib:

- wo dein Haus liegt
- deine Meinung über die Zimmer in deinem Haus
- was du gestern Abend zu Hause gemacht hast
- wo du in Zukunft wohnen willst.

Du musst ungefähr **90** Wörter auf **Deutsch** schreiben. Schreib etwas über alle Punkte der Aufgabe.

> - Write close to the word limit. If you write too much, you could introduce irrelevant details and mistakes.
> - Remember, it is important to give opinions, for example about your favourite room.
> - Make sure you use *gestern Abend* and the correct auxiliary verb (*haben* or *sein*) in the perfect tense.
> - For the fourth bullet point, say where you want to live in the future, but stick to language you know.

[16 marks]

Or Question 4.2

0 4 . 2   Dein österreichischer Austauschpartner Max fragt dich über Familienfeste. Du schreibst Max eine E-Mail.

Schreib:

- etwas über dein Lieblingsfest
- wie du deinen letzten Geburtstag gefeiert hast
- was deine Meinung über Heiraten ist
- was deine Pläne für eine Familienparty sind.

Du musst ungefähr **90** Wörter auf **Deutsch** schreiben. Schreib etwas über alle Punkte der Aufgabe.

> - The word *letzten* and the perfect tense indicate that you need to write in a past tense for the second bullet point.
> - To give an opinion about marriage, reuse the word *Heiraten* combined with a verb such as *ich finde*, e.g. *Ich finde Heiraten gut*.
> - The word *Pläne* (plans) is a hint that you will need to use the future tense to respond to the fourth bullet point.

[16 marks]

END OF QUESTIONS

Model answers and mark schemes

Practice Papers: Set 3

AQA GCSE German (9-1)

F

Foundation Tier Paper 1 Listening

Time allowed: 35 minutes
(including 5 minutes' reading time before the test)

You will need no other materials.
The pauses are pre-recorded for this test.

Information
- The marks for the questions are shown in brackets. The maximum mark for this paper is 40.
- You must **not** use a dictionary.

Advice
This is what you should do for each item.
- After the question number is announced, there will be a pause to allow you to read the instructions and questions.
- Listen carefully to the recording and read the questions again.
- Listen to the recording again, and then answer the questions.
- When the next question is about to start you will hear a bleep.
- You may write at any time during the test.
- In **Section A**, answer the questions in **English**. In **Section B**, answer the questions in **German**.
- You must answer all the questions in the spaces provided. Do not write on blank pages.
- Write neatly and put down all the information you are asked to give.
- **You must not ask questions or interrupt during the test.**
- You have five minutes to read through the question paper. You may make notes during this time. You may turn to the questions now.
- **The test starts now.**

Listen to the audio

Please note: The Practice Paper questions and answers have not been written or approved by AQA.

Section A — Questions and answers in **English**

Shopping

Gabi is planning a shopping trip.

Write the correct letter in the box.

0 1 Which shop will Gabi go to **first**?

A   B   C

[1 mark]

0 2 How will she travel into town?

A	bus
B	bike
C	train

[1 mark]

Social media

Two callers to an Austrian phone-in programme are giving their opinions about social media.

Answer the questions in **English**.

0 3 How often does the first caller use social media?

_____

[1 mark]

0 4 Which danger does the second caller refer to?

_____

[1 mark]

School life

Ahmed is talking about his school.

Write the correct letter in the box.

0 5 How many students does the school have now?

A	800
B	900
C	950

[1 mark]

0 6 What does Ahmed describe as new?

A	classrooms
B	library
C	language laboratory

[1 mark]

0 7 What does Ahmed do at break time?

A	chats
B	plays ball games
C	reads

[1 mark]

Holidays

Fabienne is talking about holiday activities.

Answer the questions in **English**.

0 8 What does Fabienne like to do in the holidays?

_____

[1 mark]

0 9 What did Fabienne do in Spain?

_____

[1 mark]

1 0 What will Fabienne do in Berlin?

_____

[1 mark]

Jobs

A caller to a Swiss radio phone-in programme is talking about his job.

Answer **both** parts of the question.

Write the correct letter in the box.

1 1 . 1 What job does he do?

A	doctor
B	office worker
C	shop worker

[1 mark]

1 1 . 2 What is his opinion of his job?

A	positive
B	positive and negative
C	negative

[1 mark]

Eating out

An Austrian teenager is talking about three restaurants where she has eaten out recently.

What does she say about each restaurant?

A	slow service
B	too expensive
C	delicious food
D	wide choice
E	nice view

Write the correct letter in the box.

1 2 Bonsai-Garten

[1 mark]

1 3 Roeckl

[1 mark]

1 4 zum Roten Tore

[1 mark]

Marriage and partnership

Three people are talking on German television about marriage and partnership.

Answer the questions in **English**.

1 5 When will the first speaker get married?

[1 mark]

1 6 What does the second speaker think of marriage?

[1 mark]

1 7 What is important about marriage for the third speaker?

[1 mark]

Birthdays

Two Swiss teenagers are talking about birthdays.

Answer **all** parts of the question.

Write the correct letter in the box.

18.1 Where does Lisa **normally** celebrate her birthday?

A	at her home
B	at a friend's home
C	at the cinema

[1 mark]

18.2 Which problem did Lisa have last year?

A	She was tired.
B	She was unhappy.
C	She was ill.

[1 mark]

18.3 When did Lisa eat her birthday cake?

A	during her party
B	later in the evening
C	the next day

[1 mark]

Future plans

Three German teenagers are talking about their plans for once they have left school.

What would they like to do?

A	do an apprenticeship
B	go to university
C	spend time travelling
D	do voluntary work
E	find paid work

Write the correct letter in the box.

1 9

[1 mark]

2 0

[1 mark]

2 1

[1 mark]

Sport

A German student is carrying out a survey about sport.

Answer the questions in **English**.

2 2 What does the first interviewee enjoy doing?

_____

[1 mark]

2 3 Why is sport important for the second interviewee?

_____

[1 mark]

2 4 Why does the third interviewee ride a bike?

_____

[1 mark]

Home town

An Austrian student, Tanja, is talking about her home town.

Which **two** statements are true?

A	Tanja lives in a small town.
B	Tanja's town has a new supermarket.
C	Tanja goes to the disco.
D	Tanja's town is popular with visitors.

Write the correct letters in the boxes.

2 5 ☐ ☐

[2 marks]

Going to the cinema

Some Swiss teenagers are talking about watching films.

What do they think of going to the cinema?

If their opinion is **positive**, write **P**.

If their opinion is **negative**, write **N**.

If their opinion is **positive and negative**, write **P + N**.

2 6 Lina   ☐

[1 mark]

2 7 Joseph   ☐

[1 mark]

2 8 Gisela   ☐

[1 mark]

Section B Questions and answers in **German**

Schulfächer

Harald spricht über seine Schulfächer.

Beantworte die **beiden** Teile der Frage.

29.1 Was ist Haralds Lieblingsfach?

A	Mathe
B	Geschichte
C	Chemie

Schreib den richtigen Buchstaben in das Kästchen.

[1 mark]

29.2 In welchem Fach bekommt Harald viele Hausaufgaben?

A	Kunst
B	Erdkunde
C	Deutsch

Schreib den richtigen Buchstaben in das Kästchen.

[1 mark]

Familie

Ilse spricht über ihre Familie.

Beantworte die Fragen auf **Deutsch**.

30 Mit wem versteht sich Ilse am besten?

_____

[1 mark]

31 Wann sieht Ilse ihre Großmutter?

_____

[1 mark]

Die Umwelt

Ingo beschreibt, was er und seine Familie für die Umwelt machen.

3 2 Was machen Ingo und seine Familie **heute** für die Umwelt?

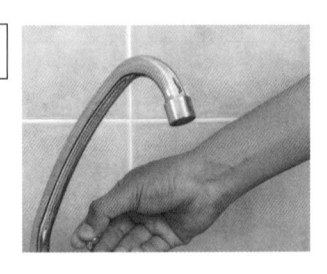

Schreib die richtigen Buchstaben in die Kästchen.

[2 marks]

Gesundes Leben

Im Radio hörst du eine Diskussion über gesundes Leben.

A	besser essen
B	weniger Alkohol trinken
C	genug schlafen
D	ins Freie gehen

3 3 Was empfiehlt die Reporterin? Schreib die richtigen Buchstaben in die Kästchen.

[2 marks]

END OF QUESTIONS

Answers and mark schemes

AQA GCSE German (9-1)

Practice Papers: Set 3

PRACTICE PAPER F

Foundation Tier Paper 2 Speaking

Time allowed: 7–9 minutes
(+12 minutes' supervised preparation time)

Candidate's material – Role-play and Photo card

Instructions
- During the preparation time you must prepare the Role-play card and Photo card stimulus cards given to you.
- You may make notes during the preparation time on the paper provided by your teacher-examiner. Do not write on the stimulus cards.
- Hand your notes and both stimulus cards to the teacher-examiner before the General Conversation.
- You must ask the teacher-examiner at least one question in the General Conversation.

Information
- The test will last a maximum of 9 minutes and will consist of a Role-play (approximately 2 minutes) and a Photo card (approximately 2 minutes), followed by a General Conversation (3–5 minutes) based on your nominated Theme and the remaining Theme which has not been covered in the Photo card.
- You must **not** use a dictionary at any time during the test. This includes the preparation time.

Teacher's scripts

Please note: The Practice Paper questions and answers have not been written or approved by AQA.

ROLE-PLAY 1

CANDIDATE'S ROLE

Part 1

Instructions to candidates

Your teacher will play the part of the waiter / waitress and will speak first.

You should address the waiter / waitress as *Sie*.

When you see this – **!** – you will have to respond to something you have not prepared.

When you see this – **?** – you will have to ask a question.

> Sie sprechen mit dem Kellner / der Kellnerin in einem Restaurant in der Schweiz.
>
> - **?** Tisch – vier Personen.
> - Sitzen – wo.
> - Getränke.
> - Im Restaurant essen – warum.
> - **!**

ROLE-PLAY 2

CANDIDATE'S ROLE

Part 1

Instructions to candidates

Your teacher will play the part of your German friend and will speak first.

You should address your friend as *du*.

When you see this – **!** – you will have to respond to something you have not prepared.

When you see this – **?** – you will have to ask a question.

> Du sprichst mit deinem Freund / deiner Freundin aus Deutschland über das gesunde Leben.
>
> - Gesund bleiben – wie (**zwei** Details).
> - Essen **und** trinken – was.
> - **!**
> - Rauchen – deine Meinung.
> - **?** Obst **und** Gemüse.

ROLE-PLAY 3

CANDIDATE'S ROLE

Part 1

Instructions to candidates

Your teacher will play the part of your Austrian friend and will speak first.

You should address your friend as *du*.

When you see this – **!** – you will have to respond to something you have not prepared.

When you see this – **?** – you will have to ask a question.

> Du sprichst mit deinem Freund / deiner Freundin aus Österreich über die Schule.
>
> - Deine Schulgebäude (**zwei** Details).
> - **!**
> - Mathe – deine Meinung (**ein** Detail).
> - Fächer nächstes Jahr (**zwei** Details).
> - **?** Lehrer.

Practice Papers: Set 3

Card A   **Candidate's Photo card**

Part 2

- Look at the photo during the preparation period.
- Make any notes you wish to on an additional piece of paper.
- Your teacher will then ask you questions about the photo and about topics related to **free-time activities**.

Your teacher will ask you the following three questions and then **two more questions** which you have not prepared.

- Was gibt es auf dem Foto?
- Was für Musik hörst du am liebsten?
- Was hast du letztes Wochenende gemacht?

Card B

Part 2

Candidate's Photo card

- Look at the photo during the preparation period.
- Make any notes you wish to on an additional piece of paper.
- Your teacher will then ask you questions about the photo and about topics related to **home, town, neighbourhood and region**.

Your teacher will ask you the following three questions and then **two more questions** which you have not prepared.

- Was gibt es auf dem Foto?
- Wirst du in Zukunft in der Stadt oder auf dem Land wohnen? … Warum?
- Was gibt es für Touristen in deiner Stadt?

Card C **Candidate's Photo card**

Part 2

- Look at the photo during the preparation period.
- Make any notes you wish to on an additional piece of paper.
- Your teacher will then ask you questions about the photo and about topics related to **life at school/college**.

Your teacher will ask you the following three questions and then **two more questions** which you have not prepared.

- Was gibt es auf dem Foto?
- Was hast du gestern in der Mittagspause gemacht?
- Wie groß ist deine Schule?

Practice Papers: Set 3

GENERAL CONVERSATION

Part 3

The Photo card is followed by a General Conversation. The first part of the conversation will be on a theme nominated by the candidate and the second part on the other theme not covered by the Photo card. The total time for the General Conversation will be between **three and five minutes** and a similar amount of time should be spent on each theme. Here is a reminder of the three themes:

- Identity and culture
- Local, national, international and global areas of interest
- Current and future study and employment

The following pages show two examples of the general conversation with accompanying commentary on how these conversations would be marked, followed by tasks.

Conversation 1: Themes 3 and 1

Und jetzt die Konversation. Fangen wir mit Thema 3 an. Beschreib deine Schule.
Das Gebäude ist alt. Die Klassenzimmer sind modern.

Magst du deine Schule?
Ja.

Was lernst du gern?
Geschichte. Der Unterricht ist interessant.

Was lernst du *nicht* gern?
Die Naturwissenschaften. Ich finde sie schwer.

Was machst du in der Pause?
Ich spiele Fußball. Ich plaudere mit meinen Freunden.

Und gestern?
Fußball.

Hast du einen Teilzeitjob?
Nein.

Wo möchtest du später arbeiten?
In der Stadt.

Welchen Beruf willst du machen?
Gärtner.

Und jetzt machen wir Thema 1. Was machst du in deiner Freizeit?
Am Abend sehe ich fern. Ich höre Musik.

Und am Wochenende?
Ich treibe Sport.

Welche Sportart treibst du?
Tennis.

Mit wem spielst du Tennis?
Mit meinem Bruder.

Wo spielt ihr?
Im Park.

Ist es teuer?
Nein. Das kostet nichts.

Gehst du manchmal ins Kino?
Ja.

Was für Filme siehst du?
Action-Filme.

Wie findest du Weihnachten?
Ich mag Weihnachten.

Warum?
Meine Großeltern kommen zu uns und wir essen zusammen.

Wie feierst du deinen Geburtstag?
Ich mache eine Party mit meinen Freunden und Freundinnen.

Was für Geschenke magst du?
Kleider.

Hast du eine Frage für mich?
Mögen Sie Karneval?

Ja, sehr.

Marks and commentary

	Communication	Range and accuracy of language	Pronunciation and intonation	Spontaneity and fluency	Total
Marks	5/10	6/10	3/5	3/5	**17/30**

The conversation has been awarded 5 marks for Communication, as only short responses are given, many of which do not include a verb. Opinions are successfully conveyed in response to the questions about school subjects. After prompting, an appropriate question is asked of the teacher-examiner, correctly using the *Sie* form of the verb. However, leaving this until the end of the conversation is risky as there will not be a second chance to ask a question if this one doesn't work.

A mark of 6 has been awarded for Range and accuracy of language as basic language and simple structures are used, such as present tense verbs. No successful references are made to past or future time frames, even though there are opportunities to do so in response to the questions *Und gestern?* and *Wo möchtest du später arbeiten?* Responding in full sentences using a verb would raise the language level of the conversation and make higher marks more accessible.

It is assumed that the pronunciation is largely intelligible but with little attempt at intonation. There may be difficulties with the umlauts in words such as *Gärtner*, *für* and *höre*, and with the *sch* and *ch* in *Geschichte*.

It is assumed that there are frequent hesitations and that delivery is generally slow. A few responses may be more fluent but the lack of intonation suggests that they have been pre-learnt. This results in a mark of 3 for Spontaneity and fluency.

> 1. Sentences can be lengthened by using connectives such as *aber*, *oder*, *also* and *weil*. Find at least one way of using each of these connectives to improve this conversation. For example, you could join the sentences *Am Abend sehe ich fern* and *Ich höre Musik* with *oder*. Take care with word order: *also* is followed directly by the verb, while *weil* sends the verb to the end of the phrase.
>
> 2. How could you develop the short responses in the first part of the conversation (the first nine questions)? For example, in response to the question *Und gestern?* you could include the structure *habe … gespielt* and perhaps add a comment about the weather, such as *Das Wetter war schön*.

Conversation 2: Themes 3 and 1

Und jetzt die Konversation. Fangen wir mit Thema 3 an. Beschreib deine Schule.
Das Gebäude ist alt, aber die Klassenzimmer sind modern. Wir haben eine neue Aula und eine schöne Bibliothek.

Was lernst du gern?
Mein Lieblingsfach ist Geschichte. Ich finde den Unterricht interessant. Der Lehrer ist auch hilfsbereit.

Was lernst du *nicht* gern?
Ich mag die Naturwissenschaften nicht. Ich finde sie schwer.

Was machst du in der Pause?
Manchmal gehe ich auf den Schulhof und spiele Fußball. Wenn es regnet, bleibe ich im Klassenzimmer und plaudere mit meinen Freunden.

Und gestern?
Das Wetter war schön, also habe ich draußen gespielt.

Hast du einen Teilzeitjob?
Nein, noch nicht. Aber ich will im Sommer arbeiten. Ich möchte Geld verdienen.

Wo möchtest du später arbeiten?
Ich möchte hier in der Stadt arbeiten. Ich will im Freien arbeiten, vielleicht als Gärtner.

Kennst du schon einen Gärtner oder eine Gärtnerin?
Ja. Mein Onkel macht diese Arbeit. Er ist sehr zufrieden.

Machen wir jetzt Thema 1. Was machst du in deiner Freizeit?
Am Abend sehe ich fern oder ich höre Musik.

Und am Wochenende?
Am Wochenende treibe ich Sport. Mein Lieblingssport ist Tennis.

Mit wem spielst du Tennis?
Mit meinem Bruder. Er spielt besser als ich, aber das macht Spaß.

Wo spielt ihr?
Es gibt Tennisplätze im Park. Das kostet nichts und ist sehr praktisch.

Gehst du manchmal ins Kino?
Ja. Ich sehe gern Filme, besonders Action-Filme. Und Sie?

Ja, ich gehe auch gern ins Kino. Wie findest du Weihnachten?
Ich mag Weihnachten. Wir haben einen Tannenbaum im Wohnzimmer. Meine Großeltern kommen zu uns und wir essen zusammen. Wir geben und bekommen Geschenke.

Wie feierst du deinen Geburtstag?
Mein Vater backt einen Geburtstagskuchen und ich mache eine Party mit meinen Freunden und Freundinnen.

Was für Geschenke magst du?
Ich mag Kleider und Schuhe.

Marks and commentary

	Communication	Range and accuracy of language	Pronunciation and intonation	Spontaneity and fluency	Total
Marks	10/10	10/10	5/5	5/5	**30/30**

The conversation scores full marks for Communication. Some extended responses are given where it is appropriate to do so, for example, when asked about Christmas, several aspects of the festival are commented on: the tree, grandparents and presents. Information and opinions are conveyed clearly and some opinions are explained, for example, why history is the favourite subject. An appropriate question is asked of the teacher-examiner, by saying *Und Sie?* in a context in which this sounds natural and makes sense.

This conversation receives 10 marks for Range and accuracy of language. There is no unnecessary repetition and a good variety of linguistic structures is used. There are some examples of complex language, such as *wenn es regnet* and several modal verbs followed by an infinitive. Connectives include *also*, *oder* and *aber*. The future is referred to successfully when talking about job aspirations, and to the past when talking about what they did during break time in school yesterday.

It is assumed that the pronunciation and intonation are generally good but with some inconsistency at times. Minor errors might include the vowel in *höre* and the *z* in *zufrieden*.

It is assumed a suitable pace is maintained, but some hesitations are made, especially in longer responses. Despite the hesitations, the conversation would still gain 5 marks for Spontaneity and fluency.

1. A good range of verbs is used, and not all are in the *ich*-form. Make a list of the verbs in other forms, such as *wir haben (eine neue Aula)* and *meine Großeltern kommen (zu uns)*. How many further examples can you add? For example, when talking about birthday presents at the end of the conversation, you could say *Meine Freunde bringen mir…*

2. In this conversation, a question is asked without any prompting from the teacher-examiner. The question is simply *Und Sie?* but this only works because it makes sense in the context. At what other points in the conversation would it make sense to ask *Und Sie?* For example, this could be used after *ich höre Musik* but not after the comment *Er spielt besser als ich, aber das macht Spaß.*

Model answers and mark schemes

…
AQA GCSE German (9-1)

PRACTICE PAPER F

Foundation Tier Paper 3 Reading

Time allowed: 45 minutes

Instructions
- Answer **all** questions.
- Answer the questions in the spaces provided.
- In **Section A**, answer the questions in **English**. In **Section B**, answer the questions in **German**. In **Section C**, translate the passage into **English**.
- Cross through any work you do not want to be marked.

Information
- The marks for the questions are shown in brackets.
- The maximum mark for this paper is 60.
- You must **not** use a dictionary.

Please note: The Practice Paper questions and answers have not been written or approved by AQA.

Section A Questions and answers in **English**

01 **My dream house**

Your German friend Angela has written a post on social media about her dream house.

Answer the questions in **English**.

> Ich möchte ein kleines Haus in den Bergen. Das Haus muss neben einem Fluss sein. Mein Lieblingshobby ist Skifahren und im Sommer will ich angeln. Ich mag die Ruhe. Im Haus werde ich keinen Fernseher haben.

01.1 Where would Angela's dream house be situated? Give **two** details.

_____

_____

[2 marks]

01.2 What does Angela say she would **not** have in her house?

_____

[1 mark]

0 2 **School and home life**

You read a blog about Sabine's life.

Write **T** if the statement is **true**.

Write **F** if the statement is **false**.

Write **NT** if the information is **not in the text**.

> Ich wohne mit meinen Eltern in einem Reihenhaus am Stadtrand. In der Schule ist mein Lieblingsfach Geschichte. Ich finde Naturwissenschaften langweilig. Fremdsprachen sind schwer.
> Am Wochenende gehe ich manchmal reiten. Ich möchte eines Tages mein eigenes Pferd haben. Ich bin ziemlich sportlich. Dienstags und donnerstags spiele ich Federball in einem Verein.

0 2 . 1 Sabine is an only child. [1 mark]

0 2 . 2 She lives in an apartment block. [1 mark]

0 2 . 3 She enjoys geography. [1 mark]

0 2 . 4 She owns her own horse. [1 mark]

0 2 . 5 She plays badminton twice a week. [1 mark]

03 Tourism

Read this advert which you see on an Austrian hotel reservation website.

Answer the questions in **English**.

> **Hotel Am Markt**
>
> Im Familienzimmer gibt es Platz für zwei Erwachsene und bis zu drei Kindern. Gegenüber dem großen Doppelbett gibt es ein Etagenbett. Kinder unter sechs Jahren können das Bett ihrer Eltern teilen. Jedes Zimmer hat Dusche und Toilette. Unser Hotel hat ein Restaurant. Frühstück ist von 7:00 bis 10:00 Uhr. Für die kalten Tage gibt es Heizung in jedem Zimmer.

03.1 How many people can sleep in a family room?

_____

[1 mark]

03.2 What is opposite the double bed?

_____

[1 mark]

03.3 What does it say about children under six years old?

_____

[1 mark]

03.4 Apart from washing and toilet facilities, what is available in every room?

_____

[1 mark]

04 Job advert

Your Austrian friend shows you this advert for a job he is thinking of applying for and asks your advice.

Read the job advert and answer the questions in **English**.

> Wir suchen Mitarbeiter für unsere Fabrik. Sie werden sechs Tage in der Woche arbeiten. Danach haben Sie zwei Tage frei aber nicht immer am Wochenende. Sie arbeiten neun Stunden am Tag. Die Mittagspause dauert eine Dreiviertelstunde. Sie dürfen die Kantine im Erdgeschoss benutzen, in der es leckeres Essen zu reduzierten Preisen gibt.

04.1 Where is the job based?

_____

[1 mark]

04.2 How many hours a day would your friend work?

_____

[1 mark]

04.3 How long would he get for lunch?

_____

[1 mark]

04.4 Where exactly is the canteen?

_____

[1 mark]

05 Relationships

Your Austrian friend shows you a dating app she has been using.

Read the extracts about what people are looking for in their partner and answer the questions in **English**.

Petra: Ich suche einen netten Mann mit Humor aber ohne Schnurrbart.

Dennis: Hunde und Katzen machen mich krank. Ich suche jemand, der keine Haustiere hat.

Lars: Gibst du deinen Sitzplatz für ältere Menschen auf? Toll! Ich kann unhöfliche Menschen nicht leiden!

Eva: Bist du witzig und geduldig? Dann will ich dich kennen lernen.

Simone: Magst du Abenteuerfilme lieber als Liebeskomödien? Dann bist du bei mir genau richtig. Gehen wir zusammen ins Kino?

05.1 What should Petra's partner **not** have?

[1 mark]

05.2 What problem does Dennis have with pets?

[1 mark]

▶ Continued

0 5 . 3 What sort of people can Lars not stand?

_____

[1 mark]

0 5 . 4 Give **one** detail about the sort of person Eva is looking for.

_____

[1 mark]

0 5 . 5 What sort of films does Simone prefer?

_____

[1 mark]

06 Social issues

Swiss school pupils were asked to list their priorities for a better society. Read their statements.

A	Es gibt zu viele Drogenabhängige.
B	Man muss Abgase in der Innenstadt reduzieren.
C	Jugendliche ohne festen Wohnsitz brauchen Hilfe.
D	Wasserverschmutzung durch Plastik zerstört das Leben im Meer.
E	Wir brauchen bessere Medikamente für Krebskranke.
F	Man soll neue Wohnungen für Flüchtlinge finden.
G	Die öffentlichen Verkehrsmittel müssen pünktlicher sein.

Write the letter of the corresponding issue in each box.

06.1 urban pollution [1 mark]

06.2 homes for refugees [1 mark]

06.3 more reliable public transport [1 mark]

06.4 improving health care [1 mark]

0 7 **Mobile phones**

Read the comments in a chat room, written by two teenagers about their mobiles.

Write the **four** correct points in the grid.

Daniel
Ich bin 12 Jahre alt. Als 10-Jähriger habe ich ein einfaches Handy ohne Internetzugang bekommen. Leider ist es jetzt kaputt, da es auf den Boden gefallen ist. Zum 13. Geburtstag werde ich endlich ein Smartphone bekommen.

Anja
Meine Eltern sagen, ab nächsten Monat muss ich einen Teil der Handykosten von meinem Taschengeld bezahlen. Das finde ich gemein! Mein Smartphone ist mein erstes Handy. Früher durfte ich nur das Tablet meiner Eltern benutzen.

	Past	Present	Future
Daniel			*will get a smartphone for his birthday*
Anja		*her smartphone is her first mobile*	

[4 marks]

08 Shopping

Read Johanna's blog about shopping.

> Das Lieblingshobby meiner Schwester ist Einkaufen und es gefällt ihr, wenn ich mitgehe. Ich sage ihr immer, dass ich keine Zeit habe. Manchmal stimmt das nicht. Ich kann es aber nicht leiden, den ganzen Nachmittag in Geschäften zu verbringen.
> Letzte Woche musste ich mit ihr ins Stadtzentrum gehen. Sie wollte neue Kleidung kaufen. Zuerst sind wir zu einem Warenhaus in der Fußgängerzone gegangen. Obwohl es viele tolle Sachen gab, war alles entweder die falsche Größe oder die falsche Farbe. Also sind wir zum Kaufhaus neben dem Brunnen gegangen. Da hat sie einen grünen Rock anprobiert. Er war sehr preiswert, weil er im Angebot war. Leider war er zu eng.
> Endlich hat sie ein T-Shirt gekauft. Wir mussten ewig Schlange stehen, bevor sie bezahlen konnte und nachher hat mein Rücken weh getan.

Which **four** statements are true?

A	Johanna loves shopping.
B	Johanna doesn't always tell the truth.
C	Johanna went shopping with her sister to buy a dress.
D	They first went to a warehouse in the pedestrian zone.
E	They went to a department store near a fountain.
F	Johanna's sister bought a green skirt.
G	The skirt was reasonably priced.
H	They had to wait in a queue to pay for the shopping.

Write the correct letters in the boxes.

[4 marks]

Section B Questions and answers in **German**

0 9 **Ein Besuch**

Lies Julias E-Mail über einen Besuch.

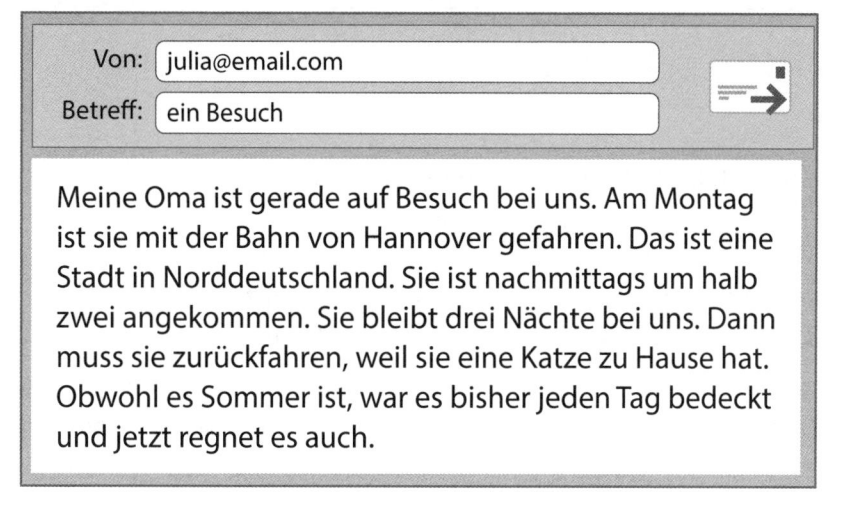

> Von: julia@email.com
> Betreff: ein Besuch
>
> Meine Oma ist gerade auf Besuch bei uns. Am Montag ist sie mit der Bahn von Hannover gefahren. Das ist eine Stadt in Norddeutschland. Sie ist nachmittags um halb zwei angekommen. Sie bleibt drei Nächte bei uns. Dann muss sie zurückfahren, weil sie eine Katze zu Hause hat. Obwohl es Sommer ist, war es bisher jeden Tag bedeckt und jetzt regnet es auch.

Schreib den richtigen Buchstaben in das Kästchen.

0 9 . 1 Julias Oma ist … gereist.

A	mit dem Zug
B	mit der Straßenbahn
C	mit dem Auto

[1 mark]

0 9 . 2 Julias Oma ist um … angekommen.

A	02:30 Uhr
B	13:30 Uhr
C	14:30 Uhr

[1 mark]

0 9 . 3 Julias Oma bleibt bis…

A	Montag.
B	Mittwoch.
C	Donnerstag.

[1 mark]

▶ Continued

09.4 Das Wetter ist…

A	angenehm.
B	heiß.
C	schlecht.

[1 mark]

10 **Schule**

Lies Walters Blog über Probleme in der Schule.

Beantworte die Fragen auf **Deutsch**.

> Letzte Woche haben meine Eltern mein Zeugnis bekommen. Es war schlecht und meine Eltern haben sich geärgert. Ich hatte eine Vier oder eine Fünf in jedem Fach. Ich will meine Noten verbessern, aber das ist nicht so einfach. Im Matheunterricht finde ich es schwer, mich zu konzentrieren. Die anderen Schüler sind immer so laut. Ich verstehe mich nicht gut mit ihnen. Sie wollen keine besseren Noten.
> Mein Bruder findet mein Zeugnis lustig. Meiner Meinung nach ist er gemein. Ich komme besser mit meiner Schwester aus. Sie macht die Matheübungen oft mit mir nach der Schule im Wohnzimmer, wenn ich Probleme habe.

10.1 Warum haben sich Walters Eltern geärgert?

_____

[1 mark]

10.2 Warum kann Walter sich in Mathe nicht konzentrieren?

_____

[1 mark]

10.3 Wie ist sein Bruder?

_____

[1 mark]

10.4 Wer hilft ihm bei den Hausaufgaben?

_____

[1 mark]

1 1 Essen und Trinken

Lies die Meinung von sechs Menschen über Restaurants und Cafés.

Carola
Hier treffe ich oft meine Freunde auf dem Weg zur Arbeit, wenn ich müde bin und einen Kaffee brauche. Ich bekomme mein Getränk sehr schnell und bleibe nicht lange. Es ist unkompliziert und auch nicht teuer.

Markus
Das Restaurant liegt nicht weit vom Fluss entfernt. Seine Spezialität ist geräucherte Forelle mit Knoblauch. Mir schmeckt das immer!

Andrea
Wir waren gestern Abend hier, um den Geburtstag meiner Schwester zu feiern. Auf der Speisekarte gab es weder Schnitzel noch Braten. Ich habe als Vorspeise eine würzige Zwiebelsuppe gegessen. Ganz lecker!

Rudi
Diese Art Restaurant gefällt mir. Ich nehme das Tagesmenü und ein Getränk, bezahle an der Kasse, setze mich hin und esse. Wenn ich fertig bin, gehe ich. Keine Kellner, kein Trinkgeld!

Benno
Wir hatten eine unvergessliche Abendrundfahrt mit Sonnenuntergang. Die Stimmung und die Musik waren toll. Das Essen hat auch gut geschmeckt.

Nico
Gestern nach dem Konzert hatten wir Hunger. Wir mussten ziemlich lange warten, weil es so viele Menschen vor uns gab. Glücklicherweise hat es nicht geregnet. Es hat sich gelohnt. Die Bratwurst mit Senf war nicht nur lecker, sondern auch günstig.

Was beschreiben die Menschen? Schreib die richtigen Buchstaben in die Kästchen.

A	ein Restaurantschiff
B	eine Imbissbude
C	ein vegetarisches Restaurant
D	ein Selbstbedienungs-Restaurant
E	ein Fischrestaurant
F	ein Stehcafé

▶ Continued

Practice Papers: Set 3

1 1 . 1	Carola	☐	[1 mark]
1 1 . 2	Markus	☐	[1 mark]
1 1 . 3	Andrea	☐	[1 mark]
1 1 . 4	Rudi	☐	[1 mark]
1 1 . 5	Benno	☐	[1 mark]
1 1 . 6	Nico	☐	[1 mark]

1 2   **Ein Märchen**

Lies diese Geschichte von den Gebrüdern Grimm.

> Ein reicher Mann wohnte in einem Schloss. Er hatte einen Sohn, der heiraten wollte. Der junge Mann war traurig, weil er die richtige Frau nicht finden konnte.
>
> Eines Abends gab es ein schreckliches Gewitter. Es blitzte und donnerte, der Regen strömte herab. Jemand klopfte an die Schlosstür. Der Alte ging selber, um sie zu öffnen. Draußen stand eine junge Frau, die Prinzessin war. Das Wasser tropfte ihr aus den Haaren, aus den Kleidern und aus den Schuhen heraus. Sie sah nicht aus wie eine echte Prinzessin.
>
> Die Frau des Alten brachte die junge Frau zum Zimmer, wo sie schlafen sollte. Am nächsten Morgen fragte die Alte: „Wie hast du geschlafen?" „Oh, sehr schlecht", antwortete die Prinzessin. „Ich habe fast die ganze Nacht kein Auge zugemacht. Das Bett war sehr ungemütlich."
>
> *Die Prinzessin auf der Erbse*

Welche **vier** Aussagen sind **richtig**?

A	Der Sohn des reichen Mannes war ledig.
B	Eines Vormittags war das Wetter sehr schlecht.
C	Der junge Mann hat die Tür aufgemacht.
D	Vor der Tür stand eine Frau.
E	Die Schuhe der Prinzessin waren nicht trocken.
F	Es war klar, dass sie eine richtige Prinzessin war.
G	Die Prinzessin hat gut geschlafen.
H	Das Bett war nicht bequem.

Schreib die **richtigen** Buchstaben in die Kästchen.

☐ ☐ ☐ ☐

[4 marks]

Section C Translation into **English**

1 3 Your German exchange partner has sent you an email.

Translate the email.

From: jens_2005@email.com
Subject: Urlaub

Jedes Jahr fahre ich in den Ferien mit meinen Eltern an die Küste. Wir schwimmen gern im Meer, wenn die Sonne scheint. Nächsten Sommer werden wir zelten. Ich schlafe lieber in einem gemütlichen Hotel.

[9 marks]

END OF QUESTIONS

Answers and mark schemes

AQA GCSE German (9-1)

PRACTICE PAPER F

Practice Papers: Set 3

Foundation Tier Paper 4 Writing

Time allowed: 1 hour

Instructions
- You must answer **four** questions.
- You must answer Question 1, Question 2 and Question 3.
- You must answer **either** Question 4.1 **or** Question 4.2. Do not answer both of these questions.
- Answer all questions in **German**.
- Answer the questions in the spaces provided.
- Cross through any work you do not want to be marked.

Information
- The marks for the questions are shown in brackets.
- The maximum mark for this paper is 50.
- You must **not** use a dictionary during this test.
- In order to score the highest marks for Question 4.1/Question 4.2, you must write something about each bullet point. You must use a variety of vocabulary and structures and include your opinions.

Please note: The Practice Paper questions and answers have not been written or approved by AQA.

0 1 Du bist auf Urlaub und schickst dieses Foto an einen deutschen Freund.

Schreib **vier** Sätze auf **Deutsch** über das Foto.

0 1 . 1
_____
[2 marks]

0 1 . 2
_____
[2 marks]

0 1 . 3
_____
[2 marks]

0 1 . 4
_____
[2 marks]

0 2 Du schreibst an deine deutsche Freundin über das Leben mit deiner Familie.

Schreib etwas über:
- Fernsehen
- Einkaufen
- Musik
- Abendessen.

Du musst ungefähr 40 Wörter auf Deutsch schreiben.

[16 marks]

| 0 | 3 | Translate the following sentences into **German**.

My father is quite old.

I often eat chips for lunch.

We don't play football every day.

My mobile phone is on the table in the bedroom.

I went to the park with my dog.

[10 marks]

Answer **either** Question 4.1 **or** Question 4.2.
You must **not** answer **both** of these questions.

Either

0 4 . 1   Du schreibst ein Blog über Sport.

Schreib:

- etwas über deinen Lieblingssport
- deine Meinung über Sport in der Schule
- was für Sport du in letzter Zeit getrieben hast
- welche Sportart du in Zukunft probieren willst.

Du musst ungefähr **90** Wörter auf **Deutsch** schreiben. Schreib etwas über alle Punkte der Aufgabe.

[16 marks]

▶ Continued

Or

0 4 . 2 Deine Freundin Emilia aus der Schweiz wird dich und deine Familie im Sommer besuchen. Du schreibst Emilia eine E-Mail über deine Region.

Schreib:

- wie du deine Region findest
- über das Wetter in deiner Region
- was du letztes Wochenende in deiner Region gemacht hast
- über deine Pläne mit Emilia für den kommenden Sommer.

Du musst ungefähr **90** Wörter auf **Deutsch** schreiben. Schreib etwas über alle Punkte der Aufgabe.

[16 marks]

END OF QUESTIONS

Model answers and mark schemes

OXFORD
UNIVERSITY PRESS

Great Clarendon Street, Oxford, OX2 6DP, United Kingdom

Oxford University Press is a department of the University of Oxford.

It furthers the University's objective of excellence in research, scholarship, and education by publishing worldwide. Oxford is a registered trade mark of Oxford University Press in the UK and in certain other countries

© Oxford University Press

The moral rights of the author[s] have been asserted

First published in 2020

All rights reserved. No part of this publication may be reproduced, stored in a retrieval system, or transmitted, in any form or by any means, without the prior permission in writing of Oxford University Press, or as expressly permitted by law, by licence or under terms agreed with the appropriate reprographics rights organization. Enquiries concerning reproduction outside the scope of the above should be sent to the Rights Department, Oxford University Press, at the address above.

You must not circulate this work in any other form and you must impose this same condition on any acquirer

British Library Cataloguing in Publication Data
Data available

978-1-38-200698-6

10 9 8 7 6 5 4 3 2 1

Paper used in the production of this book is a natural, recyclable product made from wood grown in sustainable forests. The manufacturing process conforms to the environmental regulations of the country of origin.

Printed in Great Britain by Ashford Colour Press Ltd, Gosport.

Acknowledgements

The publisher and authors would like to thank the following for permission to use photographs and other copyright material:

Photos: p23: Halfpoint/Shutterstock; **p24:** Rawpixel.com/Shutterstock; **p25:** Alexander Raths/Shutterstock; **p50:** iStock.com/vgajic; **p58(tl):** ESB Professional/Shutterstock; **p58(tm):** Ferenc Szelepcsenyi/Shutterstock; **p58(tl):** Tatiana Belova/Shutterstock; **p58(bl):** Marten_House/Shutterstock; **p58(bm):** bokan/Shutterstock; **p58(br):** BCFC/Shutterstock; **p63(bl):** happydancing/Shutterstock; **p63(bm):** BCFC/Shutterstock; **p63(br):** Rolf G Wackenberg/Shutterstock; **p67(l):** MM Studios; **p67(m):** jamalludin/Shutterstock; **p67(r):** Oxford University Press; **p68(a):** Alan Gleichman/Shutterstock; **p68(b):** Peter Bernik/Shutterstock; **p68(c):** ESB Professional/Shutterstock; **p68(d):** Tatiana Belova/Shutterstock; **p75:** ESB Professional/Shutterstock; **p76:** Monkey Business Images/Shutterstock; **p77:** Joshua Resnick/Shutterstock; **p97:** IM_photo/Shutterstock; **p100:** Rawpixel.com/Shutterstock; **p108(l):** Pressmaster/Shutterstock; **p108(m):** TaniaLerro/Shutterstock; **p108(r):** Rolf G Wackenberg/Shutterstock; **p116(a):** Jacek Chabraszewski/Shutterstock ; **p116(b):** Onjira Leibe/Shutterstock; **p116(c):** Meg Wallace Photography/Shutterstock; **p116(d):** Naypong/Shutterstock; **p121:** Phovoir/Shutterstock; **p122:** Nataliia Gr/Shutterstock; **p123:** DGLimages/Shutterstock; **p146:** wavebreakmedia/Shutterstock.

Artwork by Q2A Media (**p6(tl), p6(tm), p12, p61(tl), p61(tm), p61(tr), p61(br), p63(tl), p63(tm), p63(tr), p6(bl), and p6(br)**), Oxford University Press (**p6(tr), p61(bl), p61(bm), and p6(bm)**), Integra Software Services (**p16(tl), p16(tm), and p16(tr)**), and Garik Barseghyan/Shutterstock (**p16(bl), p16(bm), p16(br), p61(ml), p61(mm), p61(mr)**).

Every effort has been made to contact copyright holders of material reproduced in this book. Any omissions will be rectified in subsequent printings if notice is given to the publisher.